JourneyThrough™

Luke

62 Daily Insights from God's Word by **Mike Raiter**

Journey Through Luke
© 2017 by Michael David Raiter
All rights reserved.

Discovery House is affiliated
with Our Daily Bread Ministries.

Requests for permission to quote
from this book should be directed to:
Permissions Department
Discovery House
P.O. Box 3566
Grand Rapids, MI 49501
Or contact us by email at
permissionsdept@dhp.org

Design by Joshua Tan
Typeset by Grace Goh

ISBN 978-1-62707-821-4

Printed in Indonesia
First Printing in 2017

Foreword

At the birth of Jesus, angels announced to shepherds that in nearby Bethlehem there was born "a Saviour who is Christ the Lord" (Luke 2:11). This wonderful news wasn't just for those who lived in Judea 2,000 years ago, but for the whole world.

Our world is in need of salvation. We are alienated from the God who made us and loves us, and we all need to be reconciled to Him. We need someone who can bring us back to God. The good news that Luke brings to his readers is that the Saviour has come. This Saviour has made possible the forgiveness of our sins so that we can be God's friends again and, like the dying thief on the cross next to Jesus, be confident that "today you will be with me in Paradise" (Luke 23:43).

In this gospel we meet Jesus. We see His compassion for the lost. We are amazed at His authority over disease, death, and the demonic. We hear His call to surrender everything and follow Him. We learn of the salvation He has come to bring.

Journey through Luke and meet the Lord Jesus, the Saviour who is Christ the Lord.

To God be the glory,
Mike Raiter

We're glad you've decided to join us on a journey into a deeper relationship with Jesus Christ!

For over 50 years, we have been known for our daily Bible reading notes, *Our Daily Bread*. Many readers enjoy the pithy, inspiring, and relevant articles that point them to God and the wisdom and promises of His unchanging Word.

Building on the foundation of *Our Daily Bread*, we have developed this devotional series to help believers spend time with God in His Word, book by book. We trust this daily meditation on God's Word will draw you into a closer relationship with Him through our Lord and Saviour, Jesus Christ.

How to use this resource

READ: This book is designed to be read alongside God's Word as you journey with Him. It offers explanatory notes to help you understand the Scriptures in fresh ways.

REFLECT: The questions are designed to help you respond to God and His Word, letting Him change you from the inside out.

RECORD: The space provided allows you to keep a diary of your journey as you record your thoughts and jot down your responses.

An Overview

In his introduction, Luke tells us he has written this gospel so that we can be certain that our faith in Jesus rests on a firm historical foundation (1:1–4). He introduces us to Jesus, who is the Son of God, the Lord, and the Messiah. Luke's emphasis, however, is on Jesus the Saviour of the world. In her song of praise at the beginning of the gospel, Mary "rejoices in God my Saviour" (1:47). From then on we see Jesus saving sinners. This reaches its climax in the wonderful salvation of the chief tax collector, Zacchaeus, and Jesus announcing that He has come to seek and save the lost (19:10). Appropriately, the gospel ends with Jesus commissioning His disciples to take this good news of forgiveness to the entire world.

The wonderful gift of salvation demands a response of faith and obedience. The central section of the gospel (9:51–19:44) describes Jesus' journey to Jerusalem and His death on a cross. As He walks along the road, He teaches His followers about the way of discipleship. We are to follow in His footsteps as we live lives of love, mercy, and generosity. Jesus warns us that discipleship is costly and we, like Jesus, must be willing to carry the cross of suffering and rejection (14:27). Yet, glory awaits at the end of our journey, just as it did for Him. For us, it is the certain hope of Paradise (23:43).

The Structure of Luke

1:1–4	Introduction: The Purpose of the Gospel
1:5–2:52	Births of John the Baptist and Jesus
3:1–4:13	Preparation for the Ministry of Jesus
4:14–9:50	The Ministry of Jesus in Galilee
9:51–19:44	The Journey to Jerusalem
19:45–21:38	Jesus in the Temple
21:39–23:56	The Death of Jesus
24:1–52	The Resurrection of Jesus and Commissioning of the Apostles

Key Verse
"For the Son of Man came to seek and to save the lost." —Luke 19:10

Day 1

Read Luke 1:1–4

We are going to spend the next 62 days on a wonderful journey through the gospel of Luke, studying the life and work of Jesus. There is little in the Christian life more important than having confidence in the Bible. Everything we know about the life of Jesus comes mostly from the four Gospels in the New Testament. The old chorus remains profoundly true: "Jesus loves me this I know, for the Bible tells me so." Therefore, we need to be certain of the Bible's authenticity. That is why Luke begins his gospel with a prologue, a defence for the trustworthiness of all that he is about to write.

Luke was one of Paul's missionary colleagues, a friend of the apostles, and a doctor. He is writing this gospel for a noble Gentile called Theophilus, literally "friend of God". Theophilus may have been a Christian, or perhaps a seeker after God. However, no matter who Theophilus was, Luke's gospel has been written for every man and woman, both then and now.

Yes, we can trust Luke's gospel. First, because the good news he records came from the many eyewitnesses who were present. All he has written is about "things that have been fulfilled among us" (v. 1). **God promised salvation. Jesus accomplished it. Many people witnessed it. Luke has written it down for us.**

Second, we can trust Luke because he has carefully investigated everything (v. 3). A historian must be thorough and organised, concerned with both accuracy and truth. Luke assures us that there is nothing in his account that he hasn't checked, double-checked, and verified.

Sometimes we can doubt the truth of our faith. Many people dismiss Jesus, and some eminent scholars even ridicule the authenticity of the Bible. On a personal level, we may wonder if Jesus is really God's Son and our Saviour. But through his gospel, Luke is saying to us, "You can be sure!" These words are true, and you can build your life on these truths.

Sometimes, people speak of "blind faith", or of faith as being a "leap in the dark". In the light of Luke 1:1–4, are such metaphors appropriate? What do these verses tell us about the character of true Christian faith?

Why does Luke call the eyewitnesses "servants of the word" (v. 2)? What is this "word" to which Luke refers? What is it about the work of a servant that makes this description so significant?

Day 2

Read Luke 1:5–38

Appropriately, Luke begins his story of Jesus in the Jerusalem temple, God's symbolic dwelling place. The first two chapters describe, at length, the birth of two boys. It is clear from the outset that Luke wants us to contrast these two boys, as he deliberately sets their births side by side.

In both cases, the angel Gabriel announces to the parents the birth of a son. In both cases, the birth is miraculous: the first to a couple who are well past childbearing age (v. 7), and the second to a virgin (v. 27). In both cases, the parents express amazement. One child is called a prophet of the Most High (v. 76); the other, the Son of the Most High (v. 32). The parents of both sons sing to God a song of praise (vv. 46–55, 67–79). The birth of each child is described, followed by an account of his circumcision (1:59; 2:21), and finally a brief description of him growing up (1:80; 2:40).

Luke places John and Jesus side by side so that there will be no doubt as to who is the greatest. First, Luke introduces us to Zechariah and Elizabeth, godly parents whose promised child, John, will be set apart for God's service and will prepare His people for the coming of their king (vv. 5–25).

The scene then shifts about 100 kilometres north to Nazareth, where a young girl, Mary, is engaged to be married (vv. 26–38). Gabriel announces to her the birth of a son, a child of incomparable majesty. He is God's Son (v. 32) and the long-awaited descendant of King David, and will reign forever.

So far, all these two women have is the word of God's messenger. Yet they hear and believe, because they know that "no word from God will ever fail" (v. 37). We can have this same confidence as we proclaim the word of God concerning Jesus. From the very beginning of his gospel, Luke wants us to know that Jesus is unique. **He is not only the child of a virgin, but also the Son of God, and therefore deserves the obedience and worship of every man and woman.**

Compare verses
18 and 34. Both
Zechariah and Mary
question the words
of the angel. Why is
Zechariah rebuked
and Mary not?

What comfort can
we take from the
wonderful promise
that "no word from
God will ever fail"
(v. 37)?

Day 3

Read Luke 1:39–56

The angel Gabriel has announced the births of two boys. One is a prophet of God (v. 76), the other is the Son of God (vv. 32, 35). One will announce salvation (vv. 17, 76), the other will bring about that salvation (vv. 46–55, 68–75).

Even before either of these boys is born, they meet. Mary visits her relative Elizabeth, and we are told that when Elizabeth hears Mary's greeting, the child leaps in her womb. Even before he is born, Elizabeth's son has begun his ministry of pointing others to Jesus' greatness. From the moment he is conceived in his mother's womb, John is filled with the Spirit (v. 15), whose main work is to testify about Jesus (John 15:26). Later, John will introduce Jesus to the world, confessing that "one who is more powerful than I will come, the straps of whose sandals I am not worthy to untie" (Luke 3:16). This prophetic work begins even in his mother's womb!

This is something we will see again and again in Luke's gospel: people filled with the Spirit recognise Jesus and give Him all glory and honour (2:25–32, 36–38).

If a person is indwelt by the Spirit of God, the first sign of this is that they acknowledge and worship Jesus. The Spirit of God is the Spirit of Christ, and where this Spirit is present, Christ is glorified.

Mary then praises God for bringing forth the long-awaited salvation (vv. 46–55). In this wonderful song, Mary is both praising God and preaching a gospel message! Of course, that is what all great songs of praise do. Mary rejoices that in Jesus, salvation has come. As always, this salvation is welcomed by the poor and humble—those who feel their need for grace most keenly (vv. 52–53). It is the fulfilment of all the Old Testament promises, going as far back as Abraham.

Here are two model responses to Jesus. Like John, we who are God's Spirit-filled people will testify to the greatness of Jesus. Like Mary, we will worship God for His mercy in giving us, those who are spiritually poor and needy, the Saviour, Jesus.

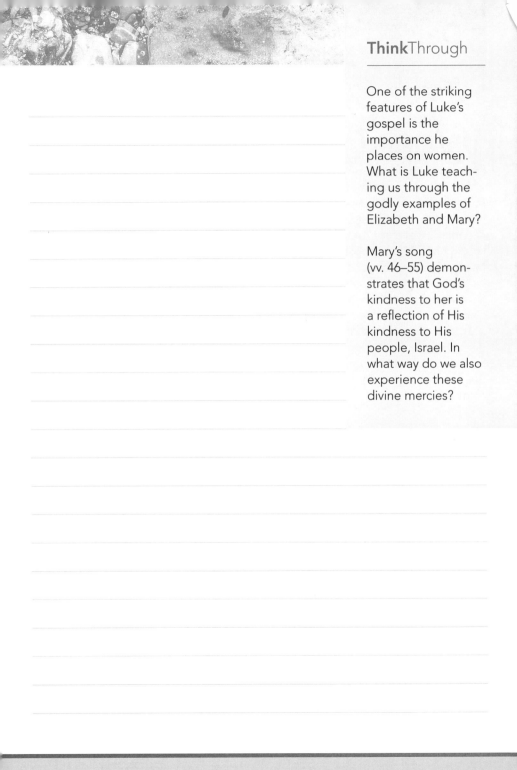

ThinkThrough

One of the striking features of Luke's gospel is the importance he places on women. What is Luke teaching us through the godly examples of Elizabeth and Mary?

Mary's song (vv. 46–55) demonstrates that God's kindness to her is a reflection of His kindness to His people, Israel. In what way do we also experience these divine mercies?

Day 4

Read Luke 2:1–21

While some aspects of the Christmas story are quite remarkable, like the appearance of the angels, Luke's account of these momentous events is rather mundane. What could be more matter-of-fact than descriptions of shepherds watching over their sheep, or of a child being born in a little Middle Eastern village?

So what happened on the first Christmas? Notice three things. First, Mary and Joseph have already been in Bethlehem for a while when Jesus was born (v. 6). He wasn't born on the night they arrived, as is commonly implied in most nativity stories.

Second, the word translated as "inn" is better rendered as "guest room" (as in Luke 22:11, where the same Greek word is found). Remember, they have gone to Bethlehem because it is Joseph's hometown. He would certainly have relatives there that he could turn to for accommodation. But by the time he arrived with Mary, "there was no room for them in the guest room" (v. 7)—probably all taken up by other returning relatives.

Third, there is no mention of a stable. Jesus was laid in a manger, which according to some biblical archaeology scholars is normally found within the confines of a village home. If this is true, then Jesus could have been born in a relative's home, because it would have been unthinkable (especially in that culture) for Joseph's family to refuse hospitality to a "brother" with a pregnant wife.

However, the important thing for Luke is not just where Jesus was born—be it a stable, cave, or house—but also who He is. Indeed, so ordinary and normal is the birth that the event would have disappeared into history, like so many other births, except that in the fields nearby, something extraordinary happens. Angels—God's messengers—appear, and give this ordinary event a most extraordinary meaning: "Today in the town of David a Saviour has been born to you; he is the Messiah" (v. 11).

"Born to you. . ." say the angels. Not just to a few shepherds, or the residents of a remote Palestinian province, but to all of us. **Today, let's look past all the accumulated layers of tradition and see the glory and greatness of God's gift, the One who is the Saviour of the world.** Then let us follow the example of the shepherds who, having seen the Saviour, "spread the word" (v. 17).

Read verses 1–2. Why do you think Luke gives us the historical setting for the story of Jesus' birth? What does this tell us about God's control of human history?

Look at verses 17–18. The shepherds were the world's first evangelists! What can we learn from them about sharing the gospel?

Day 5

Read Luke 2:22–40

The scene is 40 days after the birth of Jesus. In order to fulfil the Old Testament law's requirements for purification (Leviticus 12:1–4), Joseph and Mary take their baby to the temple in nearby Jerusalem. Here they meet two godly people, Simeon and Anna. Notice how Luke emphasises their experience in the temple and their anticipation of the coming Messiah, who will deliver Israel.

There are two great periods in the history of salvation. The first was the age of the law and the Prophets, where the focus was on Israel. If you wanted to meet God, you had to go to the temple. You had to obey the law. It was the age of promise, when Israel looked forward to its salvation.

With Jesus, a new age has dawned and everything has changed.
The old age has served its purpose of preparing for the coming of the Messiah. Now, we no longer go to a temple, or any other building, in order to meet God. We meet God by going to Jesus.

Can you see how Simeon and Anna are two symbols of the former age? They have served God in the temple.

They have devoutly kept the law of Moses. They have waited patiently for the Messiah to bring salvation. When Simeon prays to be dismissed in peace (v. 29), he is talking about both himself and the age to which he belongs. Now that salvation has come (v. 30), their work is finished. For centuries, Israel has been waiting, and now, at the appointed time, the Messiah has arrived. Simeon rejoices that Jesus is the light of the world and the glory of Israel (v. 32).

The world we live in has always been marked by darkness and shame, both morally and physically. However, Luke is reminding us that a new day has dawned. God has always been guiding the events of history to fulfil His wonderful salvation plan for all people. Just as surely as God brought the old age to its conclusion, we can be certain He will bring this "present evil age" (Galatians 1:4) to a close and reveal in glory the Lord Jesus to everyone. Then His people will enjoy the ultimate goal of all God's plans: the wonderful age to come.

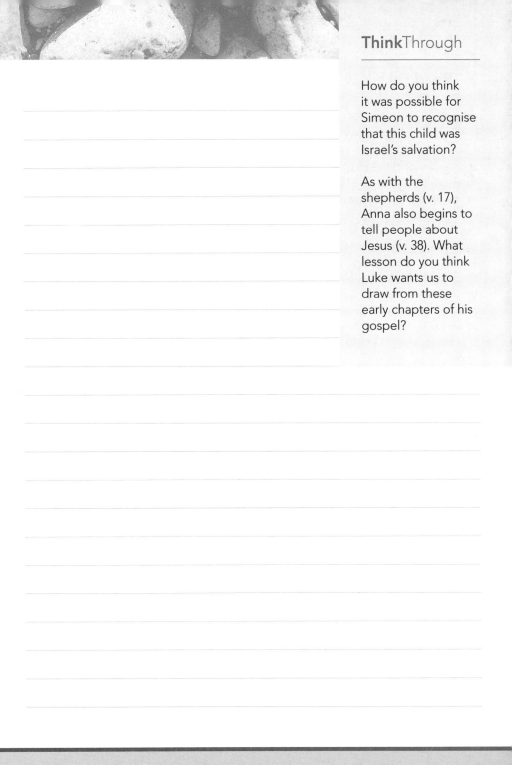

How do you think
it was possible for
Simeon to recognise
that this child was
Israel's salvation?

As with the
shepherds (v. 17),
Anna also begins to
tell people about
Jesus (v. 38). What
lesson do you think
Luke wants us to
draw from these
early chapters of his
gospel?

Day 6

Read Luke 2:39–52

Balancing love and commitment to our family with our primary obligation to our heavenly Father is often among the toughest issues we face as Christians, one that the Lord Jesus himself encountered.

Jesus had the privilege of being brought up in a family who loved and served God. His parents displayed their godliness by travelling annually to Jerusalem for the Passover. It was a 120-kilometre trip from Nazareth to Jerusalem, taking three or four days. For safety, people would travel in groups.

Jesus is 12 years old, which according to Jewish custom is the last year of childhood. Luke now presents us with a family crisis, as Jesus' parents discover on the journey home that He isn't with them. He is still in the Temple, talking with the experts in the law and leaving them amazed at His wisdom and understanding (vv. 41–47).

A worried Mary asks Him why He has caused them such anxiety. We now come to the heart of the story. For the first time in the gospel, Jesus speaks and informs His parents that His relationship with His heavenly Father must take priority (vv. 48–49). While Jesus will remain with them in Nazareth, loving, submissive, and obedient, this incident in the Temple is a turning point in His relationship with them. While they remain His parents and He their child, from now on His heavenly Father must come first.

Of course, Jesus was unique. His relationship with His heavenly Father was a special one, and His calling from God unique. Nevertheless, for many Christians, a commitment to Jesus has serious implications for their relationship with their family. We too must be about our Father's business. God's mission for the world is our mission. **God's plan to redeem the world is one that involves us all, and it must come first, even if it conflicts with our family's desires.** We still love our family, but above all, we honour our true heavenly Father.

What do we learn from this story of the uniqueness of Jesus as both the son of Mary and Joseph, and the Son of the heavenly Father?

What does it mean to "honour your father and your mother" (Exodus 20:12), especially when you are older or have left the family home?

Day 7

Read Luke 3:1–14

As Jesus preaches throughout Luke's gospel, He will repeatedly call His disciples to follow Him down a road both hard and costly. This challenge to commit to a radical lifestyle begins with the preaching of John the Baptist.

John the Baptist is one of the most important people in history. Indeed, Jesus will later say that, of all those born of women, no one is greater than John (Luke 7:28). Abraham, Moses, King David, and Elijah—John is greater than them all because he pointed most clearly to the Messiah promised in the Old Testament, especially in Isaiah 40 (see Luke 3:4–6). Luke tells us that "the word of God came to John" (v. 2). This is very important. After 400 years of virtual silence, God is speaking to His people again (Hebrews 1:1–2).

John's message is essentially the same as the prophets of old: turn your lives around, because our God and our Saviour is coming. Israel's wait was over, and so John prepares the people to meet their Messiah. However, repentance is more than just a change of attitude. It must be expressed through action. The people are to greet their coming King with transformed lives. In particular, they are to show kindness to those in need (v. 11), treat people fairly (vv. 12–13), and not abuse positions of power for personal gain (v. 14). John is not telling his listeners what they must do to be saved; he is reminding the nation—whom God has chosen and delivered from bondage—to live in response to their salvation.

John was a fiery preacher, warning people of the coming judgment. As he said, a fruitless tree is of no value to anyone (v. 9). While we live in the era of grace, we too must speak to both believer and unbeliever of the coming wrath. We cannot claim to love people and yet not warn them about God's impending judgment.

God calls us all to give sacrificially to those in need. Throughout the gospel, both John and Jesus bring this challenging word. **We who have understood and received God's grace must respond with lives that bear the fruit of justice, mercy, and generosity.**

ThinkThrough

Read Isaiah 40:1–5. When Isaiah speaks of the Lord, to whom is he referring? When John quotes this passage, to whom is he referring? What is the significance of this?

If John the Baptist were to visit your city today, what practical challenges do you think he would present to its people?

Day 8

Read Luke 3:15–23

A bride must look beautiful when she meets the groom on her wedding day. Israel is like the bride and John is getting her ready to meet her Messiah. He prepares her outwardly: he washes her, removes her dirty garments, and dresses her in proper clothes.

John's preaching has led the people to conclude wrongly that he must be the Messiah (v. 15). John corrects them and identifies two important things about the coming One. First, He is immeasurably greater than John is. In fact, John says that he is not worthy even to untie the straps of Jesus' sandals (v. 16). In Judea, teachers were held in the highest regard by their followers. As the saying went, a student must do whatever his teacher commands, except untie his sandals (a task reserved for slaves). However, says John, even that most demeaning of jobs would be too exalted for him.

Second, Jesus will baptise with the Spirit and fire, or, in other words, with the purifying, refining Spirit (v. 16). We saw yesterday that John called people to be generous and just. But how do you do that? What makes the selfish become selfless? An inner renewal and cleansing is required. **John's baptism cleansed the outside, but only Jesus' fiery baptism will cleanse the heart.**

Luke now records Jesus' baptism, which really is the formal beginning of His ministry (vv. 21–23). As Jesus is praying, He receives the authority and power for His ministry, and God gives Him a visible illustration of what this ministry will be like. The Spirit comes to Jesus in the form of a dove. It does not appear in the form of an eagle or a hawk, but in the shape of a bird that is a symbol of innocence, purity, weakness, poverty, and gentleness.

Finally, God speaks (v. 22). All people are God's offspring, but only Jesus is the eternal, beloved Son of God. There have been many great and powerful leaders throughout history, but they all have one thing in common: all are unworthy to untie the sandals of Jesus. All of us need Jesus' baptism of the Spirit and fire, and all of us must follow and worship the only Beloved Son.

We have in this passage two pictures of the Holy Spirit. The first is "fire" (v. 16). What does this tell us about the Spirit's ministry?

The Spirit then comes to Jesus in the appearance of a dove (v. 22). What does that tell us about the character of the Holy Spirit? What does it tell us about the character of a Spirit-filled Christian?

Day 9

Read Luke 3:23–4:13

Sandwiched between the inauguration of His ministry in His Spirit-anointed baptism (3:21–23) and His temptation in the wilderness (4:1–13), is a reminder of who Jesus is. Besides portraying Jesus as the legitimate descendant of David, Luke's genealogy (3:23–38) highlights the fact that all of Israel's history has been directed by God to bring about the birth of His Son. Furthermore, Jesus traces His lineage back to God's first son, Adam (3:38) but, as we'll see in a moment, where the first Adam was tempted and failed, the second and true Adam remained faithful.

Jesus is thrust out into the desert. It is the Spirit of God himself who leads Jesus to the place of testing (4:1). In each of the three temptations, Jesus' dependence on God is tested. When He is famished, will He rely on God to meet all His needs (4:2–4)? When offered a shortcut to honour and glory that avoids the cross, will He worship Satan or trust His Father to give Him all the kingdoms of the world as a reward for His obedient service (4:5–8)? And will He test God's protection by demanding some flashy display of miraculous, saving power (4:9–12)?

Of course, we too face temptations in life, but it is important to remember that Luke's gospel is the story of Jesus, and His temptations were unique. He is the one and only beloved Son of God, and so Satan puts this special relationship with His Father to the test. Where Adam, God's son, failed in Eden, and where Israel, God's firstborn, failed in the wilderness, the true, incarnate Son of God was completely obedient.

Like the ones that Jesus faced, our temptations come to us from the father of lies, who promises us things he has no authority to give. He promises us life and prosperity when all he wants is our misery and death. **Ultimately, temptation comes down to whose words you choose to believe: the lies of the devil, or the true and living word of the Father.**

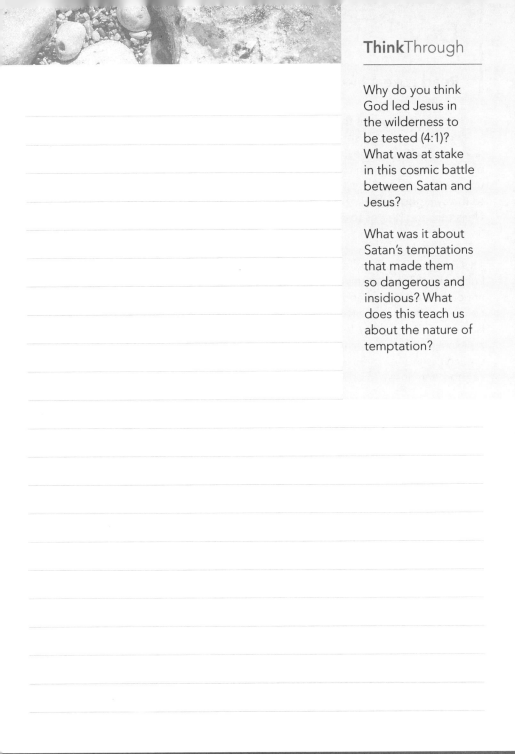

Why do you think
God led Jesus in
the wilderness to
be tested (4:1)?
What was at stake
in this cosmic battle
between Satan and
Jesus?

What was it about
Satan's temptations
that made them
so dangerous and
insidious? What
does this teach us
about the nature of
temptation?

Day 10

Read Luke 4:14–30

Jesus comes out of the wilderness, and word quickly spreads along the Galilean grapevine that one of their own has begun to teach, with unprecedented authority. Jesus goes to the synagogue in His hometown, Nazareth, and begins to preach (vv. 14–16).

This is Jesus' first recorded sermon in Luke's gospel, and in this sermon, He announces who He is and why He has come. In this sermon, an exposition of Isaiah 61:1–2 and 58:6, Jesus gives us an example of His Spirit-empowered preaching and teaching. It is a simple sermon, with just two basic points.

First, Jesus is the long-awaited Servant of the Lord, the Messiah, one who will bring salvation to Israel (v. 21). Second, the ministry of the servant is to proclaim good news to the poor (vv. 18–19). **This is Jesus' mission in a nutshell. It is about preaching, proclaiming, and announcing.** This is His first work (see v. 43). Preaching what? Freedom, liberation, and release. Luke will go on to tell us in both this gospel and Acts that the greatest liberation that Jesus both announces and effects is the forgiveness of our sins. To whom does Jesus preach this good news of forgiveness? The poor, blind, prisoners, and oppressed.

The poor are completely destitute. In the Old Testament, the term referred to both physical and spiritual poverty. The poor were the humble believers in the Lord who were utterly dependent on Him. We will meet them throughout Luke's gospel. Some are materially poor, blind, lame, or demon-possessed. Others are materially wealthy, but spiritually desperate for mercy and forgiveness. Whatever their circumstances, they come to the Saviour empty, heads bowed and on their knees, weeping, "Lord, have mercy." They go away forgiven and restored.

Today, you'll find the poor in slums and shanty towns, ordinary apartment blocks, and even mansions and palaces. Their economic circumstances may differ, but in this they are one: they know their desperate need for help, and they come to the only One who can bring them life, healing, and salvation.

Can you think of times in your own life when you've been aware of your poverty—material, spiritual, or both—and have turned in desperation to the Lord Jesus?

Jesus came to "release prisoners". What about sin makes it a kind of spiritual bondage?

Day 11

Read Luke 4:31–44

Capernaum was Jesus' base of operations for His ministry throughout Galilee. As in Nazareth, here He devotes himself to teaching and enters the synagogue. In the synagogue, He again confronts the spiritual forces of evil, this time in a demon-possessed man. Jesus has already engaged with Satan; now He confronts one of Satan's servants. The demon cries out, "Have you come to destroy us?" (v. 34). How ironic, given that destruction is the first work of Satan and his hosts. For this reason, Luke reminds us that when Jesus casts out the demon, the man is both cleansed and unhurt. Satan comes to destroy life. Jesus comes to give life (John 10:10).

The demon also bears witness to who Jesus is, proclaiming Him God's Son and the Christ, or Messiah (v. 41). Jesus silences the demon because He knows that the people hold mistaken ideas about the work the promised Christ will do when He comes. They were expecting a political liberator. Jesus must first teach them the true nature and work of His Messiahship. He has come primarily to set people free from spiritual bondage. Indeed, it will be by His death as the crucified Christ, that Jesus will demonstrate most clearly the true work the Messiah has come to do.

Jesus performed many wonders because His heart of compassion went out to the suffering. Throughout His earthly ministry, and even today, Jesus demonstrates His concern for the whole person, both physical and spiritual. However, we must not repeat the mistake of the people back then by concluding that Jesus came mainly to relieve people's physical sufferings. Even when Jesus withdraws from the crowds, they follow Him, begging Him not to leave. Jesus, though, cannot be distracted from the main work God has sent Him to do. He tells them He must go to other places to "proclaim the good news of the kingdom" (v. 43). **Preaching the gospel was Jesus' priority in His ministry.**

We live in a world of overwhelming human need. Like Jesus, our hearts must remain tender to those who are suffering, but Jesus' first work must be ours as well: to preach the good news of the kingdom.

What does it mean for Jesus to teach with authority (v. 32)? In what sense do we, or don't we, teach and minister with the same authority?

How do you balance meeting the spiritual and physical needs of people? What makes it difficult for us to maintain our priority of proclaiming good news to the poor?

Day 12

Read Luke 5:1–11

Once again, we find Jesus doing the most important work He has been sent to do: teaching the word of God (v. 1). The crowds are so large that He stands in a boat just offshore and addresses them. When He's finished, the carpenter begins to tell the fisherman how to do his job. Peter is offended that a man with relatively little experience in fishing should be giving advice to a seasoned professional. Peter knows that the middle of the day is not the time to fish; besides, after a fruitless night's labour, he knows the fish simply aren't biting. Nevertheless, Peter follows Jesus' strange command to go fishing again. The catch is enormous (vv. 2–7)!

For Peter, this is a life-changing revelation. Jesus is clearly more than a prophet. The power He exercises over the world reveals that He holds a unique authority. In that moment, Peter sees something of the glory of Jesus and, like Isaiah receiving the vision and call in the Temple (Isaiah 6:1–5), he becomes profoundly conscious of his own unworthiness

(v. 8). Yet, here is the truly amazing thing: such a humble awareness of one's sin and weakness, far from disqualifying a person for ministry, is the essential prerequisite for ministry.

Jesus tells Peter, James, and John that the rest of their lives will be spent not catching fish, but men and women (v .10). The great haul of fish they have brought to shore points forward to the thousands who will turn to Christ through their preaching.

The Lord Jesus still calls some of His followers today to leave everything and commit themselves to the greatest work of all—saving souls. **Not all of us will be frontline "fishermen", but if this is God's great work, then we must all play our part.** It is a wonderful encouragement to know, that for all the skill and experience we bring to this work, Jesus alone brings the fish into the nets. In an important sense, our work is simply to haul the fish-filled nets to the shore!

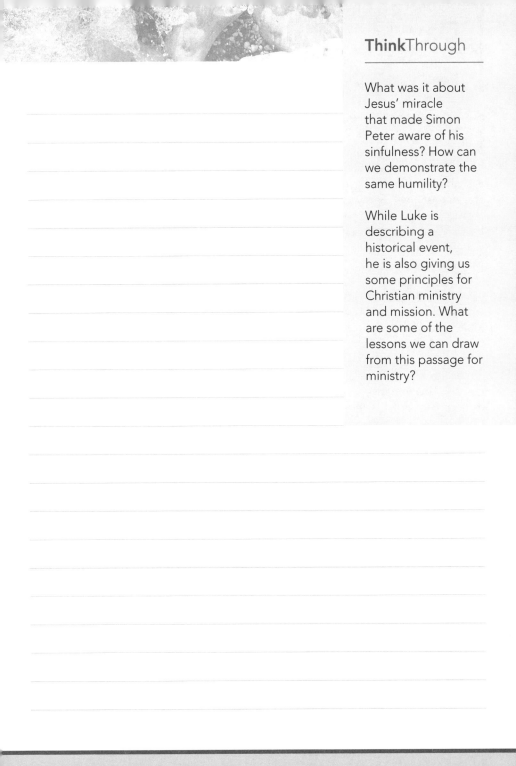

What was it about
Jesus' miracle
that made Simon
Peter aware of his
sinfulness? How can
we demonstrate the
same humility?

While Luke is
describing a
historical event,
he is also giving us
some principles for
Christian ministry
and mission. What
are some of the
lessons we can draw
from this passage for
ministry?

Day 13

Read Luke 5:12–26

In my daily prayers, I thank God for my health: physical, emotional, and spiritual. Good health is a blessing from God, and thankfully, in much of the world, people are living longer and staying healthier. Sadly, our world's report card on moral and spiritual health is far less impressive. Today, we see again Jesus' ministry to the whole person.

Jesus is continuing His ministry in and around Capernaum. Four men have a friend, or perhaps a relative, who is paralysed, lying on a stretcher. Since there is a large crowd gathered around the house where Jesus is teaching, the friends show initiative and lower him through the roof. They're desperate, bold, and a little presumptuous, but they know Jesus is the only man who can fix their friend's problem. Jesus recognises that boldness and presumptuousness for what it is: "faith" (vv. 17–19).

If the crowd were surprised at this man's unorthodox entry into the building, then they would have been stunned by what Jesus says next: "Your sins are forgiven" (v. 20).

Apart from the fact that the man was paralysed, we know nothing about him. We're not told if he was a notorious sinner, or if his paralysis was a direct consequence of any sin he had committed. Spiritually, he was no different from you or I. **Jesus, however, is showing us that sin lies at the heart of everything that's wrong with the world, and with you and me personally.** Therefore, the world's greatest need is forgiveness.

Once again, we see that while Jesus will first announce to this man the forgiveness of his sins, He does not ignore physical suffering. The paralysed man experiences both the forgiveness of his sins and the healing of his body (vv. 24–25).

Surprisingly, the religious leaders express their displeasure at Jesus' words (v. 21). They rightly recognise that He is claiming to be God. They wrongly conclude that this is blasphemy. It is not that the Pharisees cannot believe; they will not believe. From this point on, their hostility will only become more intense.

I thank God daily for good physical health, but I know that more than anything else, I need to hear His words: "Your sins are forgiven" (v. 20). And they really are!

What can we learn from this passage about the nature of faith, as expressed by the friends of the paralysed man?

In your life, how are you trying to reflect the ministry of Jesus in responding to the needs of people's bodies, minds, and souls?

Day 14

Read Luke 5:27–39

As we journey through Luke's gospel, we are constantly reminded of his main theme: Jesus is the Saviour of the world who takes away our sins (1:67–79; 2:10–11, 28–32; 3:4–6; 4:17–21, 33–44; 5:18–26). We see this again as He meets the tax collector Levi at his tollbooth (v. 27). Few men were more loathed in Israel than the tax collectors. They collected money for the hated Romans and regularly took more than they were entitled to (see Luke 3:13).

It is shocking, then, that Jesus calls a tax collector to follow Him. Levi obeys and his repentance is evidenced by the fact that he leaves "everything" (v. 28). The fact that he then hosts a banquet for his friends reminds us that he didn't sell everything he owned, but it does mean that the entire orientation of his life changed.

Religious Jews were careful about what they ate and whom they ate with. Both had to be ritually clean. By attending Levi's "party for sinners", Jesus is announcing His—and God's—love and acceptance of them (vv. 29–32).

In response to the angry Pharisees, Jesus again reminds them of the purpose of His mission. Why do you go to the doctor? Because you are unwell and can't heal yourself. People go to Jesus because they recognise they are spiritually sick. Conversely, many people do not go to Jesus because they persist in the fatal delusion that there is nothing seriously wrong with them. There is only one doctor who can cure our spiritual sickness by forgiving us, and that is Jesus.

How striking it is that Jesus' ministry was marked by "eating and drinking" (v. 33). **Dismiss any idea that Jesus was dour and overly serious. He was a man of joy who celebrated salvation.** The true killjoys are the religious leaders who again complain, this time because Jesus is always feasting. Jesus tells them His work of salvation is such a joyful thing that it must be likened to the joy of a wedding when the bridegroom claims his bride (vv. 34–35).

Surely, if Jesus' life was marked by "eating and drinking", then a mark of our life together as His people is meeting and celebrating together the joy of salvation.

What blinds people to the seriousness of their spiritual condition before God?

How can we maintain the joy of our salvation? What are some of the things that inhibit our joy?

Read Luke 6:1–16

Sabbath observance was one of the most important Jewish practices, and the Pharisees had constructed many laws to ensure that people did nothing that could be construed as work on this holy day. In both episodes here, the Pharisees have been watching Jesus and the disciples closely to see if they can catch them breaking God's law. First, the disciples are seen plucking grain on the Sabbath; they're reaping, winnowing, and preparing food, all of which are technically illegal (vv. 1–2). Then, on another Sabbath, Jesus heals a man with a shrivelled hand (vv. 6–8).

Jesus points out from the Old Testament that David permitted his men to eat prohibited food and he was not rebuked (vv. 3–4). Quite simply, the Sabbath was never intended to stop hungry people from eating; it was given for our good. Jesus exposes the spiritual bankruptcy of the Pharisees. These men are meant to be Israel's teachers, but they are ignorant of the true purpose of God's laws.

Jesus then provocatively announces that He is Lord of the Sabbath (v. 5). He has the right to determine the content and expression of God's will. **Jesus will reveal what has always been the heart and intent of the law: love for God and love for one's neighbour** (Luke 10:27).

Jesus appoints twelve who will lead His church and spearhead the spread of the gospel to all the world. The number twelve, reminiscent of the tribes of Israel, points to these men as the leaders of God's new people. They are "apostles", or "sent ones", primarily commissioned to proclaim the gospel of the kingdom.

Two things are worth noting about this diverse group of men. First, the name of Peter always heads every list of the apostles; he is both their leader and their representative figure. Second, the apostolic list as recorded in the Gospels always ends with the one called Judas, the traitor (Matthew 10:1–4; Mark 3:16–19; Luke 6:13–16).

The apostles played a unique role in God's history. Yet, all the leaders of God's people are to follow their example in teaching and modelling lives of love, and proclaiming the good news of Jesus.

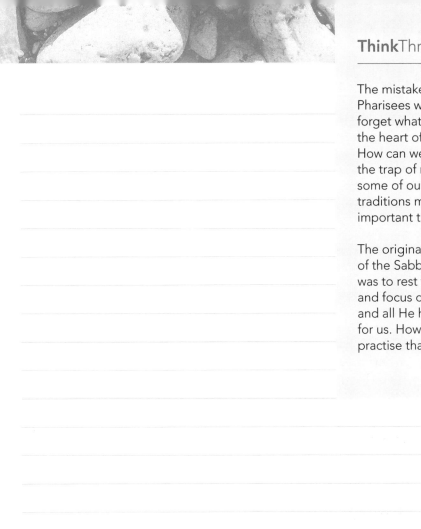

ThinkThrough

The mistake of the Pharisees was to forget what lies at the heart of the law. How can we fall into the trap of making some of our church traditions more important than love?

The original purpose of the Sabbath day was to rest from work and focus on God and all He has done for us. How do we practise that today?

Day 16

Read Luke 6:17–49

Having just called the apostles, the Lord Jesus now teaches them how to live as His disciples. Surprisingly, perhaps, He doesn't begin with a list of commands—do this, don't do that. Rather, He reminds them of their identity as His disciples, and their ultimate destiny. While His instructions are for all, His primary audience are His disciples. Who are they? They are the poor, hungry, sorrowful, and persecuted (vv. 20–22).

God's servants are essentially weak and vulnerable. They are aliens in a hostile world, and in their spiritual inadequacy, they look to the only One who can help them. But they are blessed because God will richly reward those who rely on Him (v. 23).

Conversely, those who rely on their wealth, resources, and status will be cursed (vv. 24–26). There will be a day of reversal, when God will set things right. In the coming age, those at the bottom will be honoured, the poor will be rich, the hungry satisfied, and those who weep will laugh. Conversely, those who are now on top, the rich, the well-fed, and those who laugh, will be cursed. Jesus' disciples must remain faithful.

While the response to God's grace is to "rejoice" and "leap for joy" (v. 23), there are also moral obligations. Since we've been loved, we should love others, especially those who are against us (vv. 27–36). Further, Jesus warns us not to judge others, to condemn, or to withhold forgiveness (v. 37). These three commands belong together.

In Jesus' world, if you bought some grain in the market, the seller would place your grain in a container, shake it, and get the grain to level out. Then he could put more in and press it down until it was running over (v. 38). Jesus' point is that this is how God treats us: He doesn't sell us short. He overflows with mercy. Therefore, this is how I must treat you. This is the fruit a good tree will, and must, bear (vv. 43–45). This is the life of the one whose works match their words when they call Jesus "Lord" (v. 46). This is the house that will stand on the last day when the storm of judgment comes (vv. 47–49).

Amazing grace! Overflowing mercy! How could we not respond with both joy and obedience?

What things in life make you rejoice and leap for joy (v. 23)? If the joy of our salvation has faded, what can we do to rekindle it?

Loving your enemy (v. 27) is easy to say but hard to do. How can we find the strength to love those who insult us? In the light of what Jesus says in these verses (vv.27–36), how do we practically love our enemies?

Day 17

Read Luke 7:1–17

In the synagogue at Nazareth, Jesus had announced that He had come to proclaim good news to the poor (Luke 4:16–21). Surprisingly, then, His next miracle is in response to a request from possibly the wealthiest and most powerful man in Capernaum. Yet, we have seen that poverty is also a spiritual condition. This man has a servant who is gravely ill, and for all his wealth and influence, the centurion is helpless. So, this "poor man" comes to the one with real power, the Lord Jesus (vv. 1–3).

Being a military commander, the centurion understands the chain of authority and the power of a command. He therefore grasps the power and authority of Jesus' word (vv. 6–8). Already we've heard of the people's amazement at Jesus (Luke 4:22, 36; 5:26), but now we read of Jesus' amazement (v. 9). Here is faith, not of a mustard seed, but of an oak tree, and from the lips of a Gentile. Here is genuine spiritual poverty which expresses itself in faith and humility. Then with a word, from a distance, Jesus heals the servant (v. 10).

The scene now moves 30 kilometres away, to the little town of Nain. Jesus meets the funeral procession of a young man. His death is especially tragic, because he was his mother's only son, and she had already lost her husband. In other words, here is a woman who has lost any means of support. She faces a future of abject poverty. That is why, although the Lord Jesus raises the young man, the focus of the story is the mother. Notice how Luke describes the event. She is a widow. With her is a large crowd. When Jesus sees her, He has compassion on her, and speaks to her. Then He gives the risen son back to his mother (vv. 11–17).

Jesus meets the human face of poverty and is moved by compassion. Then, with remarkable ease, like a general giving a command which is instantly obeyed, the young man sits up and returns to the waiting arms of his mother.

Jesus is stunned at the centurion's faith (v. 9). **May we all have the kind of faith that would surprise the Son of God.**

What do these two stories tell us about Jesus? What do they tell us about the people He met?

And what do they tell us about faith?

Day 18

Read Luke 7:18–35

People are continually amazed at Jesus' ministry, and so it is not surprising that the news is spreading everywhere, even to the prison cell where a faithful but perplexed John the Baptist is being held captive by Herod (Luke 3:20; 7:18–19).

John had warned Israel of imminent judgment: "The axe has been laid to the root of the trees" (3:9). He preached about the One who would bring this judgment, saying He "will burn up the chaff with unquenchable fire" (3:17). Yet, John's disciples bring him no news of signs of judgment, only works of grace (7:21–22).

A confused John sends his disciples back to ask Jesus, "Are you the one who is to come?" (v. 20). Even as they ask the question, Luke tells us of Jesus healing many with diseases (v. 21). Isaiah had foretold that when the Messiah comes, the blind will see, the deaf will hear, the lame leap like a deer, and "water will gush forth in the wilderness and streams in the desert" (Isaiah 35:5–6). In other words, John is being reminded that while judgment will come, this is the day for streams of grace, not fires of judgment.

Despite the question, Jesus reaffirms John's greatness (vv. 24–27). But stunningly, even the least of Jesus' disciples is greater (v. 28), just as the kingdom is far more blessed than the one that merely foreshadowed it. Let's never forget the incredible privilege of living under the rule of Jesus.

Finally, Jesus notes the contrasting responses of people to His and John's ministry (vv. 29–35). The religious leaders are like whining children, complaining that John and Jesus do not dance to their tune. Indeed, whatever tune these leaders play, be it happy or sad, the ministry of these two servants of God cannot please them. But the fact that the people and tax collectors have drawn near to God, through the way they have proclaimed it, shows the correctness of their teaching ("wisdom") and that they are from God (v. 35).

As you pray for family and friends to come to faith, or pray for God's blessings in your own life, it is so good to remember that these are the days of grace, mercy, and salvation.

Make a list of some of the many blessings that we enjoy today being a part of the kingdom of the Lord Jesus.

Even great saints like John the Baptist sometimes have their doubts (vv. 18–19). What can we learn about doubt and faith from John's question and Jesus' response?

Day 19

Read Luke 7:36–50

Luke now takes us into the home of a Pharisee called Simon, where Jesus is the guest of honour at a meal. This moving account wonderfully summarises much that we have already read in Luke's gospel. We see the joy of a sinner who has received mercy, and the callous heart of a Pharisee.

The dinner is interrupted when an immoral woman enters the house. Having presumably heard Jesus proclaim forgiveness, she publicly anoints and washes His feet as an expression of her love and gratitude.

Simon is silently outraged that a man thought to be a prophet should allow an unclean sinner to defile Him. Jesus then tells a little parable about two debtors (vv. 41–42). In the ancient world, to be in debt was a terrifying prospect; you faced prison or slavery. One debtor has a much greater debt than the other. Amazingly, the moneylender cancels both debts. The point is, the one who is more conscious of the size of the debt will be deeply thankful for the grace received (v. 43).

Jesus spoke in Aramaic and most likely used the word *hobha* for "sin". But *hobha* also means "debt". So, this is really a parable about two sinners, and it is obvious to everyone, not least of all Simon, about whom Jesus is talking.

The woman's spontaneous, extravagant expression of love to Jesus is a window into her heart and a measure of how much she grasps the wonder of her forgiveness (vv. 37–38, 45). In contrast, Simon's bitterness towards Jesus, displayed in how he had been rude in not greeting Jesus in the customary way of anointing and washing Him (vv. 44–45), is a sad testimony that while he knew about the God of salvation, he'd never personally experienced the forgiveness this God brings.

God has commanded us to love both Him and others. However, the Lord doesn't just give a command; He also gives the power and desire to obey it. "We love because he first loved us" (1 John 4:19). Once we've met the Saviour and experienced the liberty of having our sins forgiven, we, like this woman, can only respond with lavish praise, deep love, and open-hearted thankfulness.

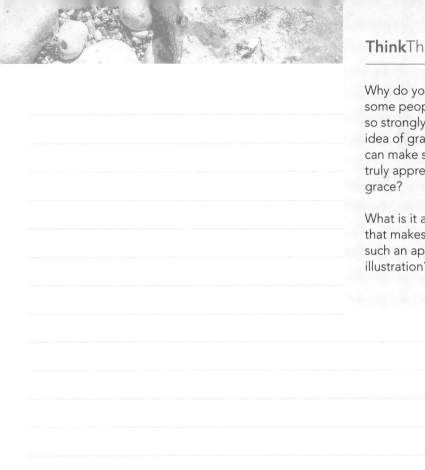

Why do you think some people object so strongly to the idea of grace? What can make someone truly appreciate grace?

What is it about sin that makes "debt" such an appropriate illustration?

Day 20

Read Luke 8:1–18

How many people attend your church? How many accepted Christ at your evangelistic service last Sunday? How many converts have you seen this year? These are valid questions, but the church can be obsessed by numbers. While this can reflect a desire to see people come to faith, it can also lead to a superficial understanding of discipleship.

We have seen how people were amazed at Jesus' teaching and miracles, and how large crowds began to follow Him (v. 4). Not everyone receives God's words in the right way, so He tells them a parable about how the different kinds of responses reveal who His true followers are.

The parable of the sower, or the soils, paints a picture of a farmer scattering seeds. The seed is God's word (v. 11). The seed falls on four kinds of ground. The first is the road (v. 12). Here, the seed has no chance to grow. It is trampled by pedestrians and eaten by wild birds. Jesus compares this to the work of Satan, who immediately stops people from hearing God's word.

Some seed fall on rocky ground (v. 13) where the topsoil is very thin. This represents those who respond enthusiastically at first, but fall away when they face opposition. Other seed fall among weeds (v. 14). These people may still call themselves disciples of Jesus, but instead of following wholeheartedly, they are distracted by the worries, riches, and pleasures of life.

Jesus has already taught the disciples that "no good tree bears bad fruit, nor does a bad tree bear good fruit" (Luke 6:43). Similarly, the good soil (v. 15) represents those followers who listen to God's Word carefully and receive it fully in faith and, since their hearts have been changed by God's Word, bear the lasting fruit of godly lives (see 6:27–42).

This insight into the kingdom of God, or God's rule through Jesus, is a gift of grace given to the disciples who earnestly seek to know the meaning of the parable. For rebellious Israel, who will ultimately reject their king, the cryptic parables hide this important revelation from them, becoming instead an expression of God's judgment: they will never fully understand His kingdom (vv. 9–10).

Let us not be distracted by the large crowds who claim to be Jesus' followers. **Let us remember that while confession is important, a life of persistent fruit-bearing is the mark of genuine discipleship.**

This parable reminds us about the importance of listening to God's Word carefully. How can we ensure, both as speakers and listeners of God's Word, that each of us "correctly handles the word of truth" (2 Timothy 2:15)?

Do you know people who might fit the description of the first three soils (vv. 12–14) described in this parable? Think about how you can pray for them.

Day 21

Read Luke 8:19–39

While crossing the Lake of Galilee, Jesus and His disciples are caught in the grip of a frightening storm (vv. 22–25). Luke contrasts the panic and terror of the disciples with Jesus' calm confidence as He sleeps. Jesus then stands up and speaks to the storm, and immediately it dies down. Psalm 107:28–29 reads: "Then they cried out to the Lord in their trouble, and he brought them out of their distress; He stilled the storm to a whisper; the waves of the sea were hushed." Jesus felt tired and slept because He was a man. Jesus ruled the winds and waves because He is God.

Jesus now enters Gentile territory and meets a man overwhelmed by demonic presence (vv. 26–37). A Roman legion contained over 5,000 men, and so by identifying himself as Legion, the man is giving us a terrifying picture of the extent of his demonic oppression.

The man spent his days naked and alone, roaming among the tombs. His life is a living death, and so how appropriate that his only companions are the rotting corpses in the graves. He is supernaturally strong; chains and ropes cannot bind him. One must never underestimate the evil power of demons (v. 29).

This story, though, isn't really about demons, but about Jesus and His powerful word. Jesus may be outnumbered by Legion, but with one commanding word, He casts the demons out. **One must never overestimate the power and authority of demons.**

Satan's hosts have only one purpose: to destroy. We see this illustrated when the demons that have been cast out immediately enter a herd of pigs and hurl them to their death (vv. 32–33). But if demons destroy, Jesus gives life. The final scene shows us the man at peace and free as he returns to society. He then becomes the first Gentile missionary Jesus sends out (vv. 35–39).

How astonishing that the people ask Jesus to leave (v. 37). Of course, this confusing response is what the apostles will face in their missionary work (Matthew 10:16–24; John 15:18–21). Everyone who brings the good news of life and peace in Jesus will meet a similar response from a world under the power of the evil one.

Verses 22–25 are a declaration of Jesus' control over the world that He, by His word, created. What comfort should this truth bring to us today?

How can we fall into the twin traps of overestimating Satan's power and underestimating Satan's power?

Day 22

Read Luke 8:40–56

Jesus has stilled a storm and cleansed a man possessed by demons. Now, He confronts humanity's last and greatest enemy: death (1 Corinthians 15:26).

The ruler of the local synagogue, Jairus, desperately pleads with Jesus to come to his house quickly; his beloved daughter is dying (vv. 41–42). Jesus agrees to come but, on the way, stops to help a woman who has suffered from bleeding (vv. 43–48). What might Jairus be saying to himself? "Certainly, her problem is serious, but she's lived with it for 12 years. My daughter has her whole life before her and is inches away from death."

Once again, we see Jesus' compassion for a woman whose condition would render her unclean (Leviticus 15:25–27). Her act of touching Jesus' garment is not some act of foolish superstition, but of faith in the power of Jesus. Despite her fear, Jesus kindly commends her faith as the kind of faith that saves, both now and forever.

Tragically, it seems, this delay has proved fatal. Jairus receives news that his daughter has died (v. 49). What must he be feeling now—pain, grief, perhaps even anger? Then Jesus brings him his greatest personal challenge: believe or despair.

While the crowds weep and wail, mocking any suggestion that the child isn't really dead, Jesus takes the parents and three disciples into her room. With the same authoritative word that calmed a storm and dismissed a legion of demons, death is banished as, with a touch of His hand, Jesus restores the girl to life (vv. 51–55).

Jesus tells those present to say nothing about this. Mind you, how could you keep such a thing secret? While He delights to bring physical life to people, Jesus knows He has an even greater work to do, and that is to bring to people the words of eternal life.

How foolish in today's world that people compare Jesus to other religious leaders and teachers. **No one else commands the forces of nature. Before no one else does all the hosts of darkness tremble and submit. Only one man has authority over life and death.** He is incomparable. No wonder they call Him the Saviour. No wonder they call Him the Lord.

You would probably not consider Jairus or the woman with the flow of blood people of great faith. Both were fearful (vv. 47, 50). What does Jesus' response to them teach us about the character of faith?

Think about the people Jesus has met and blessed over the past two chapters. What conclusions can you draw about the kind of people whom Jesus then—and now—ministered to?

Day 23

Read Luke 9:1–17

Jesus had called the twelve disciples earlier (Luke 6:12–16); now, He sends them out on a mission, giving them His power and authority to preach the kingdom and heal the sick (vv. 1–2).

It is a short-term mission into the local villages. They must travel light, with no encumbrances. Jesus warns them of the mixed response they will be sure to meet. Some will be welcomed, and this welcome will reflect the people's welcome of Jesus and His kingdom. If the disciples are rejected, they are to wipe the dust off their feet, dramatically announcing that the unwelcoming people are unclean and rejected by God. As Jews who knew the Scriptures announcing the signs of the coming Messiah, they had no more excuse for not being ready and welcoming those who come in His name.

Our situation is different: today's missionaries are engaged in a long-term ministry and may have to take many possessions with them. They normally speak to people who know nothing of God or the Bible. However, our core work is the same: proclaim the kingdom of God and that Jesus is the king (v. 2).

The only miracle of Jesus recorded in all four Gospels is the feeding of the 5,000 men—or, if you add women and children, perhaps a crowd in excess of 10,000 (vv. 10–17). As they are hungry, Jesus miraculously feeds them. All the disciples have at their disposal are five loaves of bread and two fish (v. 13). Contrast the small amount of food with the size of the crowd. Yet, Luke tells us that when they had all finished eating, they were satisfied (v. 17). Indeed, there were enough leftovers to fill twelve baskets. In the Bible, the number twelve is very significant (e.g., twelve tribes, twelve apostles). It can symbolically mean "all" or the "whole". Do you see Luke's point? The leftovers were proof of the abundance—there was still enough to feed more people.

Jesus does what only God can do: He speaks, and things come into existence. **Not only does Jesus meet our needs, but He does so lavishly.** With this confidence, we can invite our friends to come and know Jesus. Just as He deeply satisfied people back then physically, so today He will abundantly satisfy people spiritually.

Why do you think Jesus told the disciples to do the seemingly impossible and feed such a large crowd (v. 13)? What can we learn from the response of the disciples?

The Christian life is an abundant one. Think about the ways that God deals with us generously.

Read Luke 9:18–27

Imagine you have been following Jesus. You have seen Him healing many sick people, and then He has fed you a wonderful meal of bread and fish. It may appear that being a disciple of Jesus means that all your problems will be solved and life, from this point on, will be easy. Jesus quickly corrects this misunderstanding of the character of discipleship.

Jesus is aware that the presence of large crowds does not necessarily mean there is genuine faith or understanding. He asks the disciples, "Who do the crowds say I am?" (v. 18). Then, as now, people have their opinions about Jesus. Today, some say He was a great moral teacher, a deeply spiritual man, or a prophet. Jesus then turns the question on the disciples, asking, "But what about you?" Peter, speaking for all the disciples, replies that Jesus is God's Promised Ruler, the Messiah (v. 20).

Peter's reply is right, but Jesus is aware that they may draw the wrong conclusions from this. They will assume it means that the road ahead will be marked by triumph and glory. Of course, one day Jesus will reign in honour and power, but that day is not yet. For the first time, He tells them that the Messiah's road of entry to His kingdom must pass through betrayal, death, and resurrection. **Before the crown, there must be the cross. Before glory, there must be Golgotha** (v. 22).

What is true for the Master must also be true for the disciples. They must deny themselves, saying "no" to their own agendas and "yes" to the agenda of the kingdom (v. 23). If Jesus must, literally, carry a cross to enter His glory, then those who walk the road He walks must, metaphorically, do the same. They must be willing to bear ridicule and rejection.

Discipleship may even involve paying the ultimate price: one's own life. Yet, even that is a small price to pay when the promise is eternal life. The choice is stark: bear the shame of being a disciple now, or accept the world's approval and God's "shame" on the last day (v. 26).

What does it mean
for you to deny
yourself, take up
your cross, and
follow Jesus (v. 23)?

What are the
occasions when we
may be tempted
to be ashamed of
Jesus and His words
(v. 26)?

Day 25

Read Luke 9:28–50

Have you heard this popular Christian song? "Turn your eyes upon Jesus, look full in his wonderful face." If, though, you were to see Jesus, how would you respond? On a mountain, the three disciples, Peter, James, and John, are given a revelation of the awesome glory of Jesus (vv. 28–36).

As Jesus' form is changed, or transfigured, light blazes all around. Moses the great lawgiver and Elijah the great prophet appear and talk with Jesus about His approaching departure (or "exodus" in the Greek text, v. 31): His death and glorious resurrection. Then God speaks from the cloud and gives to the world His one message: "This is my Son, whom I have chosen; listen to him" (v. 35).

After every mountain comes a valley. From the high point of witnessing Jesus' glory on the mountain, the disciples are brought down to earth with a sober reminder of their faithlessness. Despite the fact that Jesus has recently given them authority to drive out demons, they lack the faith to cleanse a young boy (vv. 37–41). Luke spares us no details in describing the destructive effects of the demon's presence in the boy:

he screams, convulses, and foams at the mouth. In the harshest words Jesus uses about the disciples, He recalls God's anger and frustration with His unbelieving people, Israel, in the wilderness (v. 41; Numbers 14:11; Deuteronomy 32:5, 20). They are an "unbelieving and perverse generation". Luke does not tell us how the disciples' faithlessness expressed itself. Were they intimidated by the seriousness of the boy's condition? Had they begun to put confidence in their own abilities? What a contrast, though, between their impotence and the power of Jesus' word: He speaks and the boy is made well (vv. 42–43).

Just as God remained faithful to fickle Israel throughout her history, the Lord Jesus shows grace and patience in staying with the disciples. Their greatest betrayal is still to come! He again reminds them that He will be "delivered into the hands of men" (v. 44). Of course, it will be one of the Twelve that eventually betrays Jesus.

How quickly our faith can turn to fear, our praise to perversity. Let's keep turning our eyes upon Jesus, and our ears to His words of life.

What is the significance of Jesus, Moses, and Elijah discussing Jesus' departure or exodus (v. 31)? What does that tell us about the importance of His death and glorious resurrection?

Why is it that in our lives, high moments of spiritual joy can often be followed by low troughs of doubt and despondency?

Day 26

Read Luke 9:51–62

Jesus has now set His face to go to Jerusalem (v. 51). This will be His final journey, and in that city He will meet opposition, betrayal, trial, death and, ultimately, resurrection. The next ten chapters of Luke's gospel (10–19) are full of statements about "going", "following", and being "along the road".

These chapters record more than just Jesus' journey to Jerusalem. Certainly, "the road" (v. 57) refers to the road Jesus walked on, but it is also a metaphor for Christian discipleship. That's why, as He walks along the road, Jesus is continually teaching about discipleship. Indeed, followers of Jesus were initially called followers of "the Way" (Acts 9:2).

The most direct route from Galilee to Judea is through Samaria. For centuries, Jews and Samaritans had despised each other and so, not surprisingly, a Samaritan town rejects Jesus. Jesus rebukes the disciples for wanting to bring judgment on them. They haven't yet understood that Jesus is going to Jerusalem to die on a cross that He might save people from their sins, not judge them for their sins (vv. 51–56).

The work of proclaiming the kingdom requires single-minded devotion and, as He has already told the disciples, a life of self-denial. This is illustrated in three dramatic encounters that Jesus has "along the road" (v. 57). First, an enthusiastic follower expresses his wish to follow Jesus anywhere and everywhere. I wonder if he really understood where Jesus was going; none of the Twelve seemed to. The next two men want to first fulfil family obligations before following Jesus. In each case Jesus reminds them, and us, of the uncompromising character of discipleship. He is not laying down new commands, such as "don't own a house" (v. 58). He is not overturning the command to honour one's parents. Jesus himself instructs us to care of our families (Matthew 15:4–6). **Jesus is dramatically emphasising that following Him is the priority and that will sometimes involve costly choices** (vv. 60–62).

Many Christians throughout history have given up homes, careers, comfort and even, for a time, family in order to serve the kingdom. God may not call on all of us to make such sacrifices, but He does call all of us to be willing—He demands our total commitment.

Our Master, the Lord Jesus, had nowhere to lay His head (v. 58). What do you think that means for us practically?

Can you think of times when there might be tension between doing the work of the kingdom and fulfilling one's family responsibilities?

Day 27

Read Luke 10:1–24

We have just heard Jesus tell would-be disciples how costly it will be to follow Him. Now, He sends out 72 and repeats some of the instructions He gave earlier to the Twelve (Luke 9:1–6).

Jesus announces that it is harvest time (v. 2). You don't need many labourers for sowing, but you need them at harvest time. Jesus is announcing that the days of promise for Israel are over, and now each person must individually respond to the coming of the Messiah (v. 16).

Proclaiming the gospel to a hostile world can be dangerous. Jesus announces, "I am sending you out like lambs among wolves" (v. 3). A shepherd's job is to protect the sheep, but here Jesus is announcing that He is sending them into the part of the field where the wolf pack prowls. Sheep are weak and wolves savage. What a stark picture of Christian mission. The Book of Acts records the many sufferings the apostles faced. Today, thousands of Christians are in prison or suffering because they boldly preach Christ. Of course, our Good Shepherd is always with us, but a commitment to gospel preaching is a commitment to suffer.

The 72 return triumphantly from their successful mission (v. 17), but Jesus reminds them not to lose perspective. First, they should not be surprised at their authority over demons. Indeed, Jesus saw the ultimate downfall of Satan (v. 18). Satan is the great serpent (Genesis 3; Revelation 20:2) and here Jesus similarly describes his demonic followers as snakes and scorpions (v. 19). He's not referring to literal snakes, as the disciples have just come back and seen the demons subject to Jesus' name. He is speaking of our triumph over the forces of darkness.

Second, Jesus reminds us that greater than seeing success in our Christian ministry is the unspeakable joy of knowing that before the foundation of the world, God picked up His pen and wrote our names in His book of life (v. 20). **It is wonderful when people are blessed through your ministry, but more thrilling is that God has set His eternal love upon you.**

What causes Jesus joy? Read verses 21–22. Why is God's grace to the humble such a cause of joy for Jesus?

What causes you joy? What are some of the ways in which we can rekindle or deepen the joy of our eternal salvation?

Day 28

Read Luke 10:25–37

The Lord Jesus has just thanked His Father for hiding the truths about the kingdom of God from the "wise and learned" and revealing them to "children" (v. 21). Luke records a parable of Jesus to illustrate this point.

An expert on the law, trying to trap Jesus, asks, "What must I do to inherit eternal life?" (v. 25). Jesus affirms the expert's understanding of what is required: to love both God (Deuteronomy 6:5) and one's neighbour (Leviticus 19:18). He tells the expert, "Do this and you will live" (v. 28). Aware that he cannot fulfil the law's demand, the scribe tries to justify the lack of love for his neighbour by asking, "Who is my neighbour?" The Lord Jesus then tells a story about a man who made the 28-kilometre journey downhill from Jerusalem to Jericho, a road notorious for robbers. He was beaten and left for dead. A priest and a Levite, who knew that the law required them to care for the poor and oppressed, ignored the man.

Why did they keep on walking? Did they fear ritual contamination, or the return of the thieves? Jesus doesn't tell us. He simply says that they walked by on the other side. In another parable, the Lord sternly condemned such behaviour: "I was thirsty and you gave Me no drink; I was . . . naked and you did not clothe Me" (Matthew 25:42–43 NKJV). To this He could have added, "[I was] lying beaten by the side of the road and you walked on by".

Then along came a Samaritan, despised by Jews for being a half-caste and spiritually compromised. Yet, while Jewish teachers hardened their hearts, this man demonstrated God-like compassion. This is what made the story so shocking for the original hearers: that the one who understood and grasped the intent of the law, and expressed his love for God through love for his neighbour, was the outcast. Note the thematic link to Jesus' earlier words, "not the wise and learned but the child".

Under both the old covenant and the new, faith in and love for the God who has saved us is expressed through performing deeds of love.
"What must I do?" asked the man. "Imitate the one who did mercy," Jesus said to him. To all of us Jesus says, "Go and do likewise." This is the revealed truth of God.

ThinkThrough

What are some of the "games" we play to justify ourselves so that we don't have to express costly love?

Who is your neighbour? What can you do today to express love to someone, especially someone outside your circle of friends?

Day 29

Read Luke 10:38–42

Jesus continues on His journey to Jerusalem. He arrives, with His disciples, in the village of Bethany less than 3 kilometres away from Jerusalem (John 11:18).

Jesus comes to the home of a family He knows well. There are two sisters, Mary and Martha, who live in this particular home. They have a brother, Lazarus (John 11), but he plays no part in this story. The sisters are both disciples of Jesus. They have welcomed Him into their home as a demonstration of welcoming Him into their hearts (vv. 5–7). The gospel has met their spiritual needs and so they, in turn, meet the physical needs of those who bear this gospel.

One sister, Martha, is serving the guests, and there were probably many of them, and the other is taking the opportunity of Jesus' presence to sit and listen to Him. Whom will Jesus commend? Anyone hearing this story for the first time would assume that Martha would be commended and Mary rebuked. After all, Jesus has just told a story about a Samaritan who put his faith into action.

Once again, Jesus surprises us. While Martha has been expressing her love for Jesus practically, the work has begun to overwhelm her and distract her from what she needs to focus on. Mary, though, has understood what is at the heart of discipleship—taking time to listen to the word of Jesus. Remember God's words at the Transfiguration: "This is my Son, whom I have chosen; listen to him" (Luke 9:35). Jesus has made it abundantly clear: only one thing is needed (v. 42). **Jesus is not dismissing Martha's good work as unimportant; however, the wise disciple will not let the good take the place of the best.**

Recently, my wife asked our four adult children how their daily Bible reading was going. It is a very important question. If we have let the busyness of life—even busyness in the Lord's service—distract us, then we need to remember that "few things are needed—or indeed only one" (v. 42).

Read 2 Timothy 3:14–17. What do these verses tell us about the importance of God's Word, and the impact it can have on our lives?

How are you doing in your daily Bible reading? What changes do you think you may have to make in the light of Jesus' words?

Day 30

Read Luke 11:1–13

The important things in the personal life of a disciple of Jesus are Bible reading and prayer. Having just encouraged us to "listen to Jesus", we are now given teaching on prayer.

John the Baptist had taught his disciples how to pray and, so, Jesus' disciples want to learn how to pray a "Jesus kind of prayer" (v. 1). Jesus begins with a model prayer (vv. 2–4), and then to further explain the meaning of prayer, He tells a parable (vv. 5–8). Finally, He concludes by reminding us of the essence of prayer (vv. 9–13).

The Lord's Prayer is remarkable for its brevity. First, we are to pray for the honour and glory of God, and for the spread of His rule across the world (v. 2). Then, we pray for the Father to grant us our needs: daily bread, forgiveness, and God's protection in times of trial (vv. 3–4).

The parable describes a man who has a guest drop by at midnight (vv. 5–8). To his embarrassment, the host cannot feed his guest because the cupboard is empty. So he goes next door and wakes up his neighbour, who eventually grants the request, giving him "as much as you need" (v. 8).

Perhaps one reason we don't go to our heavenly Father with our needs is that we think that our "cupboard" is full. We forget how destitute we are. In both the model prayer and the parable, Jesus shows us that prayer is about asking (v. 8). The one in need and who has nothing comes to the One who has plenty and who gives out of His abundance. In both cases, a key petition is the request for bread: one metaphorical, the other literal.

Jesus concludes by reminding us of the essential nature of Christian prayer. We should not be reluctant to ask, seek, and knock (v. 9). God will give us as much as we need. We may not always receive what we think we need, but God will give what is the very best for us because He is the good and loving Father. In particular, the Father will give us His Spirit: the One who empowers us for world mission, enables us to honour the Father's name, and conforms us to the image of Jesus. What better thing is there to ask for?

How should we let the Lord's Prayer (vv. 2–4) shape the way we pray as individuals and as a church?

The man in the parable asked his neighbour because his cupboard was empty. What stops us from praying as often as we should?

Day 31

Read Luke 11:14–28

On His way to Jerusalem, Jesus gives a man born mute a voice for the first time, and the crowds are amazed (v. 14). However, as we will see, "amazement" can be positive or negative.

First, some accuse Jesus of being in league with Satan (v. 15). They wickedly claim that His ministry is destructive. A man has just been set free and filled with joy, and some call it demonic.

Jesus points out the logical absurdity of this accusation. If, by Satan's power, He is defeating Satan's own hosts, then Satan is fighting against himself. No, what Jesus is doing is destroying the hold Satan has on people. We have just seen one of Satan's captives, locked up in a prison cell of lifelong silence until Jesus breaks in, overpowers the jailer, and sets the man free. What He has done with this man is a picture of His whole ministry (vv. 17–20). Supremely, it will be through His death and resurrection that Jesus will defeat Satan and set His people free.

You will notice that the context here is one of warfare. Jesus uses military language because Christians are involved in a spiritual battle. When you are at war, the question of whose side you are on is black and white. "Whoever is not with me is against me", says Jesus (v. 23).

Another danger in spiritual warfare is that of aligning yourself with Jesus but not continuing with Him (vv. 24–26). According to ancient tradition, demonic spirits preferred to live in a host, like a person or an object, rather than have some independent existence. Jesus refers to this in verses 24–26. His point is simple: if God has set you free from any affliction, you can't remain empty or neutral towards Him. The right response is to fill this emptiness with His Holy Spirit, or else another spirit will move in.

In this passage, Jesus is warning against the dangerous belief that a person can maintain a stand of neutrality when it comes to Jesus (v. 23). **Ultimately, the choice is a blunt one: the one who does not follow Jesus follows Satan.** Anyone who is not a friend of King Jesus is, in the end, an enemy of King Jesus. Whose side are we on?

ThinkThrough

What amazes you about the Lord Jesus? How can we ensure that we never lose that sense of wonder?

What evidence can you see of people today still calling the good works of Jesus and His followers evil or demonic?

Day 32

Read Luke 11:29–54

We have just seen that a person is either for Jesus or against Him. Many people, however, think they can sit on the fence. They neither curse Jesus as demonic nor worship Him. They reserve judgment until there is more evidence.

We meet such people in our passage today. They have already asked for a sign (v. 16), but Jesus calls them a wicked generation (v. 29). They have already been given many signs. The pagan people of Nineveh were not given any sign (except for Jonah, who served as a sign to them), and neither was the Queen of the South, yet the preaching of Jonah and the wisdom of Solomon were enough to produce faith in them. The power and authority of Jesus' words and works are far greater, so the demand for a sign is just another mark of their unbelieving hearts (vv. 29–32).

Jesus has taught the truth openly like someone who lights a lamp (v. 33). Why would you need more light when light is already flooding the room? If, though, your view of Jesus is warped, then you show yourself to be in spiritual darkness (vv. 35–36).

The battle with the religious leaders continues as Jesus denounces their hypocrisy. Jesus catalogues their failures as the teachers and leaders of God's people: they lack integrity because what you see on the outside does not match what is on the inside (vv. 39–41); they neither teach nor live out justice and mercy, which are at the heart of a godly life (v. 42); they crave the adulation of people (v. 43); they teach spiritual life but lead people into a spiritual graveyard (v. 44); and they make God's law an unbearable burden for people, without the comfort of grace (v. 46).

Most seriously of all, they stand in the tradition of their forefathers who opposed and murdered God's true messengers. What they did to the prophets, they now will do to the One who is greater than all the prophets combined (vv. 47–51).

There is a word here to Christian leaders: do not let your life and words become a barrier to people finding salvation, but let them be a bridge to Jesus instead (v. 52). There is a word to us all: **walk with grace and humility, and remember that the only heart you should judge is your own.**

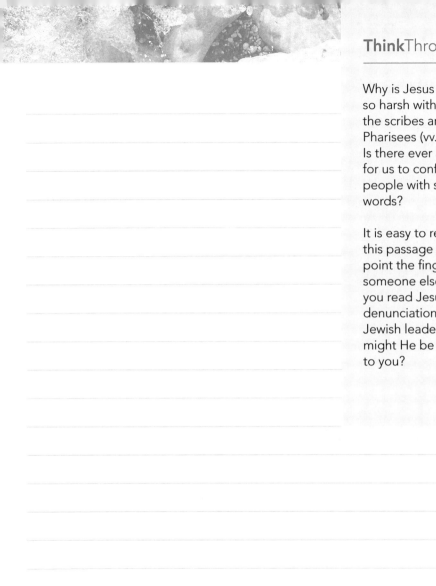

Why is Jesus
so harsh with
the scribes and
Pharisees (vv. 39–52)?
Is there ever a time
for us to confront
people with such
words?

It is easy to read
this passage and
point the finger at
someone else. As
you read Jesus'
denunciations of the
Jewish leaders, what
might He be saying
to you?

Day 33

Read Luke 12:1–34

After His denunciations of the Pharisees, Jesus now warns His disciples against hypocrisy. One day, everything will be made known, even the secrets and desires of the heart, and so we should live now with that Judgment Day in mind (vv. 2–10).

While Jesus is preaching, a man asks Him to arbitrate in a dispute with his brother over their inheritance (v. 13). This man is a living example of the hypocrisy Jesus has just warned people against. On the outside, it appears he wants justice, but Jesus publicly exposes the greed that is in his heart (vv. 14–15).

Jesus then tells a parable about a man who did not understand the purpose of life. He was so obsessed with amassing his possessions that he gave no thought to his mortality and that one day he would have to give an account of his life before God (vv. 16–21).

Most people place too much importance on gaining money and possessions, and for selfish purposes. Jesus calls us to a radical reorientation of our thinking.

He notes that life is about being rich—towards God (v. 21). Life is about His kingdom and storing up treasure in heaven (Matthew 6:20; Luke 12:33, 18:22).

This has two implications. First, we should not worry (vv. 22–31). God is concerned that we have the necessities of life and, just as He cares for the birds and the flowers, we can trust Him to care for us. Second, being "rich towards God" means using our wealth to care for the needs of others (v. 33). Jesus will repeat this theme on His journey to Jerusalem (Luke 16:9, 19–31; 19:8, 13).

Jesus is not saying that we shouldn't save and invest. He would not be against buying a house. However, He is saying that these are secondary things. A wise disciple will listen to Jesus' words seriously and fearfully. Do you truly obey Him? **One day, the secrets of our hearts— and our bank balances— which we have kept hidden away, will be revealed.** So, let us live lives of trust and generosity.

ThinkThrough

Jesus warns against "all kinds of greed" (v. 15). Greed results in spiritual damage. Can you identify some of the different kinds of greed in life?

It is not always easy to trust God to meet our daily needs (vv. 22–31). What stops us trusting Him? How can we encourage each other to trust in the generous heavenly Father?

Day 34

Read Luke 12:35–48

When I was a young Christian, I regularly faced the temptation to live like my non-Christian friends. One thing that kept me from compromising my Christian commitment was the fear of God. God's love and grace are powerful motivators for continuing to serve Jesus faithfully, but so is a godly fear of the coming judgment (see vv. 4–5).

Having addressed how we should use our possessions, Jesus now speaks about our ministry to one another (v. 35). The picture He paints of our life together is that of the extended household. The Master is the Lord Jesus, who is to be unquestioningly obeyed, and we are His servants. The Master has been away and these parables describe how His servants should behave in His absence (vv. 36–40).

Jesus says, in effect: live like there is no night-time. It may be midnight, but stay in your work clothes so that when the Master comes, we can be sure we are ready to greet Him (v. 36). In other words, live in a constant state of preparation for His return. Then, in one of the most remarkable pictures of the humility of Jesus, the King portrays himself as serving the servants (v. 37). What an astonishing picture of our Servant King, and our heavenly hope!

When the Master returns, He will reward those who have been serving Him faithfully (vv. 42–44). However, the focus of the parable is on the faithless servants (vv. 45–47).

Jesus will treat each of His servants individually and fairly. The servant who wilfully abuses any authority the Lord has entrusted to him will incur God's wrath. The servant who knows the Master's intention but does not fulfil it will receive a greater judgment. The one who is ignorant of Jesus' will receives a lesser judgment. Clearly, there will be different levels of judgment, for "God 'will repay each person according to what they have done'" (Romans 2:6). While the precise details of judgment may not be clear, we know the main message: be found faithful.

Let us remain confident of the salvation won for us by Christ on the cross, but let's not presume upon His grace by not living faithfully until He comes.

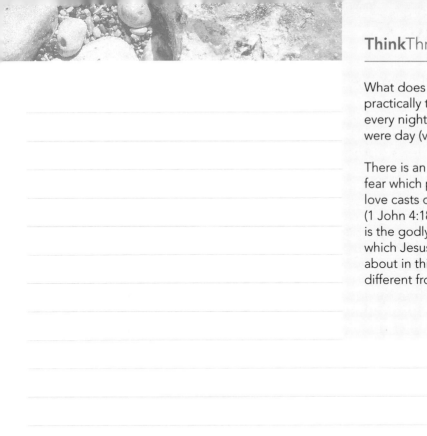

What does it mean practically to live every night as if it were day (vv. 38–40)?

There is an ungodly fear which perfect love casts out (1 John 4:18). How is the godly fear which Jesus speaks about in this chapter different from that?

Day 35

Read Luke 12:49–13:9

I hope you see the importance of reading the whole of Luke's gospel. Some of Jesus' teachings were hard to hear, both for ancient Israel and for us today. However, if we are to truly understand the message and mission of Jesus, we need to hear everything He said, including the more confronting words, like those in today's passage.

Fire purifies by separating the good from the bad. Jesus' ministry always has that effect. Inevitably, loyalty to Christ will impact even our closest relationships (12:51–53); we have to choose to follow Christ because of who He is. Yet people, especially the Jewish people of Jesus' day, had no excuse for not following Jesus. The signs that He is the long-awaited Messiah were even clearer than the weather reports (12:54–56).

When it comes to Judgment Day, people can make two mistakes. One is to fail to act now. Today is the day to be reconciled to God. It will be too late when you stand before the Magistrate (12:57–59). The other mistake is to think it won't happen to me, because I'm not as bad as some other people. No, says Jesus, we all need to repent (13:1–5).

Jesus was firstly addressing Israel (13:6–9). In the parable of the fruitless fig tree, He reveals that God has been incredibly patient with His faithless people over many centuries, but now, His patience is running out. The widespread rejection of Jesus only further demonstrates the depth of their sin and the seriousness of their predicament. While God will not completely abandon His chosen people (Romans 9–11), Jesus will soon send His disciples to others who are more responsive to His gospel.

We are halfway through Luke's gospel and this is a good opportunity for us to pause for self-reflection, to avoid repeating the mistake of Israel. Have we understood who Jesus is? Have we confessed our sins and turned away from them? Have we been reconciled to God? Are we sure we will be declared righteous when we stand before the heavenly Magistrate?

God longs to forgive us and bring us into His eternal kingdom. Now would be a very good moment to ensure that we are in a right relationship with God and have a certain hope of eternal life. If we have done what Jesus says, then thank God for saving us!

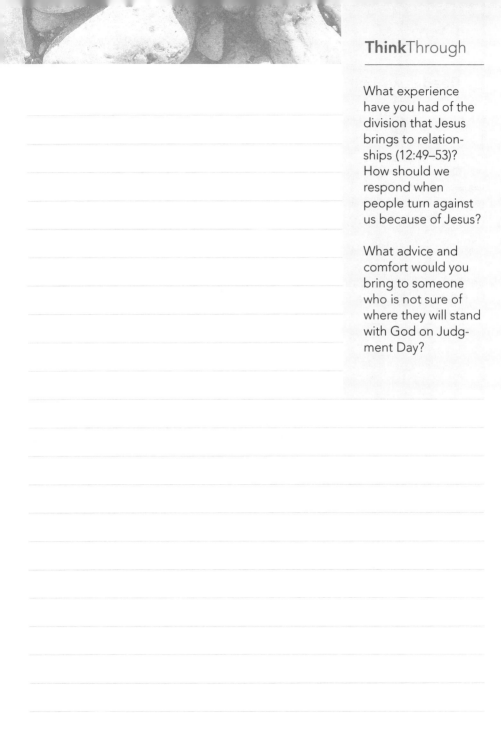

What experience have you had of the division that Jesus brings to relationships (12:49–53)? How should we respond when people turn against us because of Jesus?

What advice and comfort would you bring to someone who is not sure of where they will stand with God on Judgment Day?

Day 36

Read Luke 13:10–35

In 1 Timothy 4:16, Paul exhorts his young co-worker: "Watch your life and doctrine closely." Timothy is not to be so consumed with other issues that his own spiritual welfare is neglected. Jesus offers a similar warning here.

Despite all He has done and taught, Jewish religious leaders still fail to understand the character of God's kingdom. Jesus wonderfully heals a woman who has been crippled by a spirit for 18 years (v. 11). Rather than rejoicing at Jesus' power and grace, a synagogue leader complains because He has performed this good deed on the Sabbath. Jesus rebukes him for his hypocrisy. There is no more appropriate day to do good than on the Sabbath (vv. 14–16).

Jesus then tells two parables to make the point that God's kingdom must grow (vv. 18–21). What has begun as a small and inconspicuous movement will become universal and very visible. It will grow to include those outside of Israel. The fact that God's kingdom will embrace Gentiles is in itself a judgment on the unbelieving Jews. The last will be first, and the first, last (v. 30).

A man then asks Jesus how many will be saved (v. 23). Jesus tells him to worry first about his own salvation, because many who expect to be in the kingdom will find the door shut (v. 25). Isaiah 25:6 describes the age to come as a wonderful banquet of food and drink. Sadly, though, many of God's people who think they will be there will find themselves excluded, while around God's table will be the Gentiles (v. 29). Jesus rejoices that Gentiles will come to Him but is deeply grieved that many of His own people have rejected Him (vv. 31–35).

We have already seen Jesus eating with sinners (Luke 5:30; 7:34), and this picture of salvation as a banquet will be repeated on Jesus' lips (v. 29). The surprising thing is who will be there. There will be a poor woman oppressed by a demon, not a hypocritical synagogue leader. There will be those who have been the last, not those who have been the first (v. 30).

Jesus says, "Make every effort to enter through the narrow door" (v. 24). **While we should be concerned about the salvation of others, let us first watch our own life and ensure that we will be seated at this heavenly banquet.**

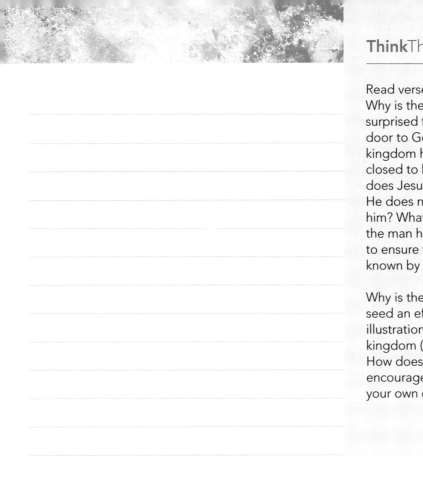

ThinkThrough

Read verses 24–27. Why is the man surprised that the door to God's kingdom has been closed to him? Why does Jesus say that He does not know him? What could the man have done to ensure that he is known by Jesus?

Why is the mustard seed an effective illustration of God's kingdom (vv. 18–19)? How does that encourage you in your own context?

Day 37

Read Luke 14:1–24

My wife and I enjoy having guests over for a meal. Of course, the purpose of sharing a meal is much more than the consumption of food. It is the context for the expression of love and acceptance. As we saw in chapter 13, meals will play an increasingly important part in Jesus' teaching about the kingdom.

Chapter 14 opens with Jesus being invited to a meal in the home of a Pharisee (v. 1). Jesus again raises the issue of proper observance of the Sabbath, and the silence of the Pharisees (vv. 4, 6) shows their continued refusal to see what God is doing in Jesus.

Jesus then uses the example of meals to teach an important lesson, not just about humility, but also salvation (vv. 7–11). To choose the best seat at a dinner, next to the host, is to display pride. Clearly Jesus is talking not just about human relationships, but also about how we see ourselves before God. **We are gravely mistaken if we believe we deserve to sit next to God. Salvation is by grace to the humble and undeserving.** Once we understand this, then we will love and accept others who are undeserving (vv. 12–14).

The final parable paints a powerful picture of the history of salvation (vv. 15–24). It is the story of a man who invites guests to his banquet. Initially, they accept the invitation, but when the banquet is ready, they make excuses. It appears the excuses are flimsy. You examine a field or cattle before you buy them. Being newly married does not stop you from attending any social functions. The master then invites outsiders to fill his banquet table.

The guests who have been invited first are the Jewish people, who largely refuse God's invitation into His kingdom. The poor and those on the country lanes are the sinners and the Gentiles, who warmly receive salvation.

While this is a parable, meals are still powerful expressions of love. It is not surprising that the Lord Jesus commands us to keep having a meal together as a way to remember His death for us (Luke 22:14–20). Church meals should be important contexts both for deepening our life together and for welcoming outsiders into our midst.

Meals are an important way to express Christian love. How important are these kinds of meals in your family life? How about in your church life?

What flimsy excuses do people make today for not accepting God's offer of salvation?

Day 38

Read Luke 14:25–35

Some years ago, I went to work in a country that had a reputation for not being safe. I took my wife and two small boys. A Christian friend said to me, "How could you take your children to a place like that? I would never do that." Actually, we considered it a privilege to take our children to that country. However, my friend's comment troubled me. Didn't she understand that the decision to follow Jesus Christ is a costly one, and may even have implications for the family?

In this passage, Jesus teaches that He must have first place in our lives. This means He has priority over our families (v. 26). When Jesus calls us to "hate" our families, He is being deliberately provocative. We are still to lovingly fulfil our obligations to our families. One of Jesus' last acts was to ensure the well-being of His mother (John 19:26–27). However, following Him may involve costly family decisions.

Following Jesus involves carrying a cross (v. 27). For Jesus, this was literal. For most of us, it will be metaphorical. To carry a cross is to walk a road that leads to death.

Jesus is saying that we may be called upon to make great sacrifices for the sake of Him and His kingdom. Are you ready for that?

The final two parables exhort us to seriously think through what following Jesus may mean for us (vv. 28–33). In many countries, the decision to become a Christian is a life and death choice. We need to ensure that enquirers into Christianity know exactly what opposition and suffering they might face if they become a Christian.

Jesus' final warning reminds us that a disciple who is not willing to make the tough choices or persevere with Jesus when things get tough, is like salt that is no longer salty (v. 34). It is useless.

While it is not easy to follow Jesus, we must remember all that Jesus has done for us. In love, He offers us salvation free of charge. In love, He has given His own life so that we might be forgiven and reconciled to God. In love, He tells us, before we commit our lives to Him, what discipleship will involve.

Before you became a follower of Jesus Christ, did someone tell you what it would involve? Why do we sometimes seem reluctant to do that?

What advice about the cost of disciple-ship would you give to someone who wants to become a Christian?

Day 39

Read Luke 15

Once again, Jesus eating with sinners provokes an angry response from the Pharisees (v. 2). In Luke 15, Jesus explains why He has meals with sinners.

Jesus tells three parables about a lost sheep (vv. 4–7), a lost coin (vv. 8–10), and a lost son (vv. 11–32). They all make the same point: anyone who loses something valuable, upon finding it, will celebrate joyfully. The heavenly Father rejoices when sinners repent and turn back to Him, and Jesus reflects this in eating and drinking with them.

The third and climactic parable is emotionally powerful (vv. 11–32). The loss of a sheep or a coin is incomparable to the loss of a son. Therefore, the father's joy is extravagant (vv. 22–24). However, this final parable has a surprising conclusion. With the introduction of the older brother, Jesus directly addresses the Pharisees who, like this brother, show their anger at the grace of the Father (vv. 25–32).

The older brother is furious that his father has welcomed his wicked son back (v. 28). "All these years I've been slaving for you," he says. This revealing comment shows how little he understands the character of his father.

The Old Testament law demanded that a rebellious son be stoned (Deuteronomy 21:18–21). The brother wanted judgment, not grace.

The father had two sons out of relationship with him. One is a prodigal son and the other a proud son, yet he treats both sons the same. He goes outside to each one and speaks words of grace. His final words are a rebuke to the older brother: "We had to celebrate and be glad" (v. 32). **To complain about God's grace is to stand against God's plan to save sinners.**

The parable does not tell us how the older brother responded, although it is surely significant that the brother who was outside the house at the beginning of the parable is now inside, and the one who spent years living there is now outside (v. 28). The first shall be last and the last, first (Luke 13:30).

The human heart is naturally disposed against grace. "That's not fair!" we cry when someone receives something undeserved, particularly when we feel that we deserved it instead! That is why grace is so amazing.

What does the parable of the prodigal son (vv. 11–32) teach us about the character of true repentance?

Have there been times when you resented God's graciousness to other people? How can we better reflect God's grace in our dealings with people?

Day 40

Read Luke 16:1–9

In Ephesians 4:28, Paul tells the thief to stop stealing and work. Why? "That they may have something to share with those in need." God blesses us financially so that we can be a blessing to others. This is colourfully illustrated in this parable of the shrewd manager.

Many people find this a difficult parable because Jesus seems to commend a man even though he acts dishonestly. A rich man has entrusted his manager with all his wealth. However, the master is told that the manager has been squandering his property (it is the same word previously used to describe the squandering of the prodigal son). The master sacks him. The manager now needs to find other people to provide for him. There are some men who are in great debt to his master. The manager does them an enormous favour and reduces their debts. He hopes that they will be so grateful that when he is fired, "people will welcome me into their houses" (v. 4).

It seems the manager has been dishonest. Indeed, Jesus calls him "unrighteous" (v. 8 NASB). Of course, Jesus is not condoning his method of making friends, but He is commending his shrewdness in understanding the importance and purpose of money in this age. This man understands that in our world, money can buy things like security, friendship, and a future.

Jesus draws a lesson for His followers from this manager. We know that owning "worldly wealth" (v. 9) is a part of living in this world, but we also know that it will pass away with this world. Therefore, while we have it, we are to use it to make friends. But here is the significant difference: we make friends for eternity.

In his letter, James rebukes the wealthy believer who offers no help to a poor brother in ragged clothes (James 2:15–16). For both Jesus and James, how we help our needy brothers and sisters has eternal consequences. In our church, there may be a single mother who can't pay the rent, a sick brother who can't afford a doctor, or an unemployed father who can't feed his family. **If God has given us the financial resources, then we need to bless such people, and so make friends for eternity.**

What do most people think is the purpose of having money? How is the Christian perspective radically different?

What does Jesus mean by this picture of "making friends for eternity"? Can you think of anyone in need right now that you could bless in this way?

Day 41

Read Luke 16:10–13

Repeatedly in Luke's gospel, Jesus warns us against the dangers of wealth. In these next verses, He emphasises the importance of the right use of money. It can be the measuring stick of our commitment to Him. If we cannot be faithful with "worldly wealth", how can we be faithful with other things (vv. 10–12)? In other words, the way a person uses their money and possessions is a reflection of their entire life orientation.

Jesus has already told people to store up treasures in heaven (Luke 12:33–34). He says the same thing here when He warns us against being unfaithful with money (v. 11). If, like the rich fool (12:16–21), we store up our wealth and neglect the poor and needy, then "who will trust you with true riches", which are the riches of heaven?

Jesus is not denying the importance of faith in Him, but He is reminding us that faith must express itself in works. James says: "Suppose a brother or sister is without clothes and daily food. If one of you says to them, 'Go in peace; keep warm and well fed,' but does nothing about their physical needs, what good is it? In the same way, faith by itself, if it is not accompanied by action, is dead" (James 2:15–17).

Jesus then portrays money as a slave owner who has complete control over a person (v. 13). **Money is deceptively powerful— when people think they are using their money, their money is actually using them.** That is easy to prove: if I am the master of my money, then I can happily give it away. But if money is my master, it controls me.

A little later in the gospel, Jesus meets a rich ruler and offers him heavenly treasure if he gives away his money (Luke 18:18–25). Surely heavenly treasure is infinitely more valuable. But the man cannot do it, "because he was very wealthy" (18:23). Who was the master in that relationship: the man or his money?

It is often said that when it comes to money, the important thing is our attitude. That is only half true. A right attitude must express itself in practical generosity. If I am poor, I need more than someone's right attitude.

ThinkThrough

If God has "entrusted" worldly wealth to us, what does this tell us about who the true owner of our wealth is, and how we should use it?

Why do you think Jesus speaks so often about the dangers of greed and the importance of generosity?

Day 42

Read Luke 16:14–18

There is no denying that Jesus' teaching on money is challenging and uncompromising. Both then and today, many find this teaching hard to hear. And the more people love their money, the stronger will be their opposition to Jesus' words. That is why the sneering response of the Pharisees (v. 14) betrays the darkness of their hearts: they are lovers of money.

The Pharisees took pride in the fact that they were concerned for the Law, but their opposition to Jesus demonstrates that they do not understand the true intent of the Law. This is what Jesus addresses in these next few verses.

We saw on Day 7 that John the Baptist's ministry marked the turning point of the ages. He was the last of the prophets of the old covenant, but his preaching announced the beginning of the new age under the rule of the Messiah. It is an age where there are no barriers to anyone coming into the kingdom and verse 16 in today's passage literally means, "Everyone is strongly urged to enter it". **But the call to enter the kingdom is also a call to live by the values of the kingdom.**

All that Jesus taught about living by the values of His kingdom is consistent with the Old Testament Law. His teaching isn't abolishing the Law. Rather, by His teaching, He is showing what the Law really expects of people.

Traditionally, two areas of obedience to the Law which highlight most clearly the genuineness of a person's relationship to God are money and fidelity. What were the great sins of Israel in the days of Malachi? They gave to God sacrifices that were second-rate and damaged, and they divorced their wives (Malachi 1:8, 2:16). We can also see this later on in a parable that Jesus tells about pride and humility, where a Pharisee boasts that he is neither greedy nor an adulterer (Luke 18:11).

Following Jesus and pleasing God is, on the one hand, so simple. Love is the fulfilment of the law. Love your neighbour by living a life of material generosity, and love your husband or wife through lifelong devotion. On the other hand, it is also demanding, and only possible by God's saving grace and power. Yet those who love like this can be assured of heavenly blessings.

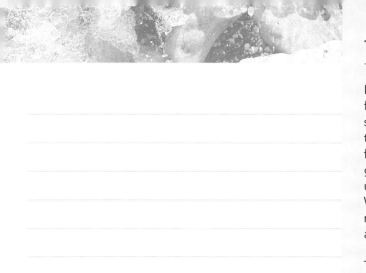

Reflect on the
fact that there is a
spiritual dimension
to both money and
fidelity. Money is a
god who beckons
us to trust it (v. 13).
What is it about
money that makes it
a God-substitute?

The Old Testament
often likens idolatry
to spiritual adultery.
How is an idolater
like an adulterer?

Day 43

Read Luke 16:19–31

In the previous parable (vv. 1–9), Jesus told us to use our money to bless others so that we might be "welcomed into eternal dwellings" (v. 9). The next parable explains what this means (vv. 19–31). It is a frightening and compelling story which shows how serious the issue of the right use of money is.

We meet two men whose lifestyles are completely different. One is extravagantly rich and the other unspeakably poor. This is the only parable in which Jesus gives a character a name. The poor man is called Lazarus, which means "God helps". While he is physically poor, he is spiritually rich. Jesus has already announced, "Blessed are you who are poor, for yours is the kingdom of God" (Luke 6:20). This is Lazarus.

In that same passage, Jesus said that those who are hungry and weep now will be full and will laugh in the age to come, while the well-fed now will be hungry then (6:20–26). This is what we see after the deaths of these two men. While Lazarus is in bliss in paradise, the rich man is in agony in hell. He should have demonstrated his faith in God by using his worldly wealth to bless Lazarus.

The rich man's final request is for someone to warn his brothers, who also walk past the poor and needy with the same hardness of heart that he did (vv. 27–28). Abraham tells him that they have been warned. The law says, "If anyone is poor among your fellow Israelites . . . do not be hard-hearted or tight-fisted towards them. Rather, be open-handed and freely lend them whatever they need" (Deuteronomy 15:7–8).

The rich man then begs that Lazarus be returned from the dead to warn them. Abraham's answer is the right one: they have the Scriptures (v. 31).

We have these same Scriptures today, both the Old Testament and New Testament. More than that, we have the wonderful example of our Lord and Saviour. Paul reminds us of the grace of Jesus, who "though he was rich, yet for your sake became poor, so that you through his poverty might become rich" (2 Corinthians 8:9). **Let us pray for the grace and strength to live generously, that we may be welcomed into eternal dwellings.**

Think about who might be the Lazarus at your gate.

Having read these two parables from Luke 16, what decisions will you make about your money and possessions?

Day 44

Read Luke 17:1–19

The 19th-century Russian novelist Fyodor Dostoevsky wrote about humanity, "If he is not stupid, he is monstrously ungrateful. Phenomenally ungrateful. In fact, I believe that the best definition of man is the ungrateful biped." By contrast, thankfulness is one of the great marks of the disciple of Jesus.

Jesus begins this section with some brief teaching on different aspects of discipleship. There is the warning not to bring about the ruin of another person's faith (vv. 1–3), and then teaching about forgiveness, faith, and the recognition that we should see serving Jesus as our duty, as well as our joy and privilege (vv. 4–10).

Luke then records Jesus entering a village where He meets ten lepers (vv. 11–19). They have heard that Jesus is passing through and, with excitement and anticipation, seek Him out. They speak to Him "at a distance" because leprosy was more than a physical illness; it meant social and religious isolation. Jesus doesn't heal them right there and then. He gives them a test of their faith. Without feeling or looking any different, they believe Jesus' word and on their way to the priest, "they were cleansed" (v. 14).

Now we come to the point of the story: ten men experience the grace and power of Jesus, but nine continue on their way. Ten are happy that they have been healed, but only one is grateful, and he spontaneously lifts up his voice in praise to God. Once again, Luke shocks us—"and he was a Samaritan" (v. 16). Jesus has repeatedly announced that it will be the sinners and the Gentiles who will enter the kingdom first.

The climax of the story comes with Jesus' final words to this man: "Get up and go your way. Your faith has saved you" (v. 19 LEB). Ten men were healed, but only one was saved. **Ten men experienced the physical and earthly blessings of God, but only one received the spiritual and eternal blessings.** His thankfulness is a demonstration of the genuineness of his faith.

Psalm 30 would be the song of the Samaritan, and you and me:

"You have turned my mourning into dancing; you have taken off my sackcloth and clothed me with joy, so that my soul may praise you and not be silent. O Lord my God, I will give thanks to you forever." (Psalm 30:11–12 NRSV)

What is the benefit of recognising that "doing our duty" is an important aspect of Christian discipleship?

Take a few moments and "count your blessings". What can you thank God for today?

Day 45

Read Luke 17:20–37

The church has often been obsessed with questions about Jesus' return. We search for clues as to where and when. Jesus now corrects many misunderstandings about the coming of the kingdom. He reminds the people that the real issue is not "when" it will come, but "who" will bring it in. The answer is Jesus himself, who is standing in their midst (v. 21).

Jesus now describes the character of His coming. First, there will be no ambiguity about the coming of the Son of Man. At His first coming, Jesus arrived almost unnoticed in a humble Galilean village. People were unsure and asked, "Isn't this the carpenter's son? Isn't his mother called Mary?" (Matthew 13:55). Next time, the coming of Jesus will be unmistakable. It will be worldwide, sudden, and inescapable (v. 24). Just as the hovering of vultures tells you that death is nearby, so just as certainly the coming of the Son of Man will announce that the time for judgment has come (v. 37).

Jesus then tells His disciples that the coming of the Son of Man will be sudden. In the days of Noah and Sodom, judgment came when the wicked did not expect it. There were two kinds of people going about their daily routines of sleeping, eating, drinking, marrying, buying, and selling. **Outwardly they looked the same, doing the same things, but one was ready for the coming judgment and one was not.**

What was the difference between the two people? "Remember Lot's wife" (v. 32). Lot and his wife lived in Sodom and spent their days doing similar activities. However, unlike his wife, while Lot lived in Sodom, Sodom did not live in him. Peter says that Lot "was tormented in his righteous soul by the lawless deeds he saw and heard" (2 Peter 2:8).

In other words, those who are not prepared for Jesus' coming are those who try to "keep their life" (v. 33). This life is more important to them than the life to come. While their daily activities look the same, those who are ready for the coming of Jesus have a very different focus and commitment.

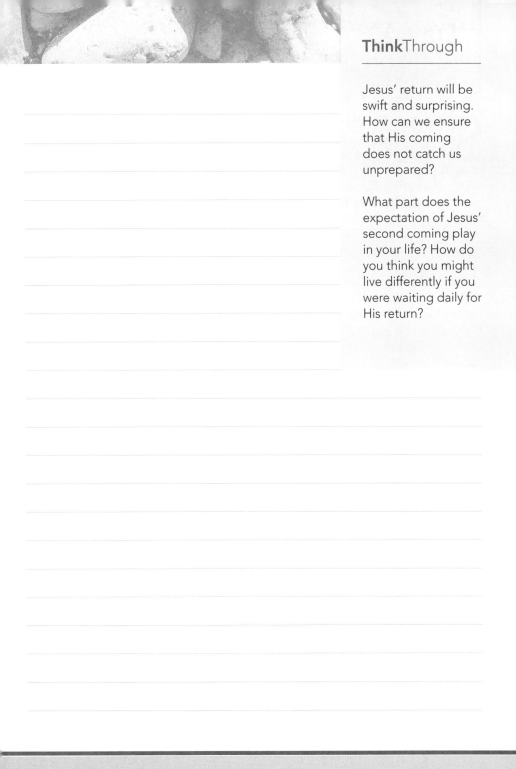

Jesus' return will be swift and surprising. How can we ensure that His coming does not catch us unprepared?

What part does the expectation of Jesus' second coming play in your life? How do you think you might live differently if you were waiting daily for His return?

Day 46

Read Luke 18:1–8

Some time ago, a friend of mine was being cruelly and unfairly harassed by people who wanted to do him harm. In his despair, he wrote, "I do not know what to do except pray. I have eternal life and I am spiritually in peace, but I am very depressed and upset." When we suffer like this, we long for Jesus to come and establish His just rule over the world.

Having taught His disciples about His return (Luke 17:20–37), Jesus now tells a parable about how they should live while they wait for Judgment Day. There are two characters in the parable, a hero and an adversary.

First, we meet a judge. His work is to ensure that the wicked are punished and the innocent are vindicated. However, this judge has become insensitive to the suffering of other people. He neither fears God nor cares about people (v. 2).

The judge is approached by a needy and vulnerable widow. Widows are regularly presented in the Bible as models of faith and faithfulness (e.g., 1 Kings 17:7–16; Mark 12:41–44), for the essence of faith is a recognition of one's deep need and utter dependence on the Judge of all people. This woman, with apparently no one to represent her, pleads her case for justice before this callous judge.

The judge's response is as predictable as it is inexcusable: he dismisses her. Yet she returns day after day. Finally, the judge relents so that, literally, "she won't come and give me a black eye" (v. 5).

The lesson Jesus wants us to draw from this story is that we, too, should keep praying and not lose heart. **If an unjust judge will give a widow justice, how much more will the just and loving heavenly Father grant justice to His faithful people?**

In a world which is opposed to the gospel and where there is so much injustice, it is easy for believers to lose heart and think that God does not care. However, even when it appears God is not acting, we should keep trusting Him and praying. He will bring justice quickly.

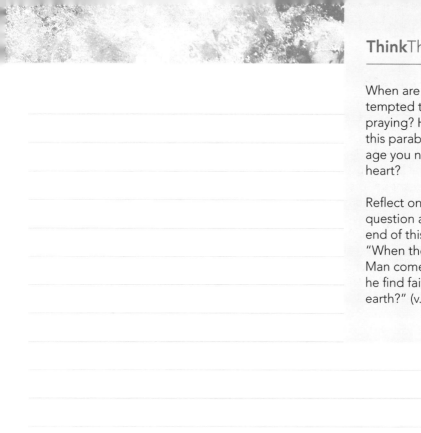

When are you tempted to give up praying? How does this parable encourage you not to lose heart?

Reflect on Jesus' question at the end of this parable: "When the Son of Man comes, will he find faith on the earth?" (v. 8)

Day 47

Read Luke 18:9–43

As our children get older, most of us would encourage them to be independent. We want them to think for themselves and not be so reliant on us to care for them. Such advice, though, is not appropriate when it comes to our relationship with God. As we saw with the persistent widow (Luke 18:1–8), God blesses the dependent who express their need of Him.

Jesus tells a story of a Pharisee who boasts in his own virtues and expresses no reliance on God (vv. 9–14). Then a tax collector comes to God with his hands empty. Yet he is the one who leaves right with God, for it is the humble who rely on God, who are exalted.

Then parents bring their children to Jesus, and He announces that unless we become like a little child, we will never enter the kingdom (vv. 15–17). He is not speaking about the innocent faith of children. He is talking about the essential mark of a child. Little children are dependent on their parents for everything: life, food, protection, home, and clothing. Their parents are the centre of their world, and the children are helpless without them.

That is why a child is the model of those who belong to the kingdom: they are helpless and completely dependent on their heavenly Father.

Jesus then meets a rich man who, like the Pharisee in the parable, affirms his goodness (vv. 18–21). Jesus tells him to give all his money to the poor. Of course, if he sells everything he owns, he will become dependent, like a little child. But he cannot do it. Again, we see that it is those who exalt themselves, who will be humbled.

Finally, Jesus meets a blind beggar (v. 35). If the rich man had everything you could want, this man had nothing. He knows all about dependence, for he spends his days begging. This man, with nothing to offer, asks Jesus for his sight and is given salvation. The humble are exalted.

Jesus is reminding us that the values of God's kingdom are not those of the world. The world esteems the rich, important, and independent. God exalts the least, the beggar, the dependent. Remember, we must become like a little child.

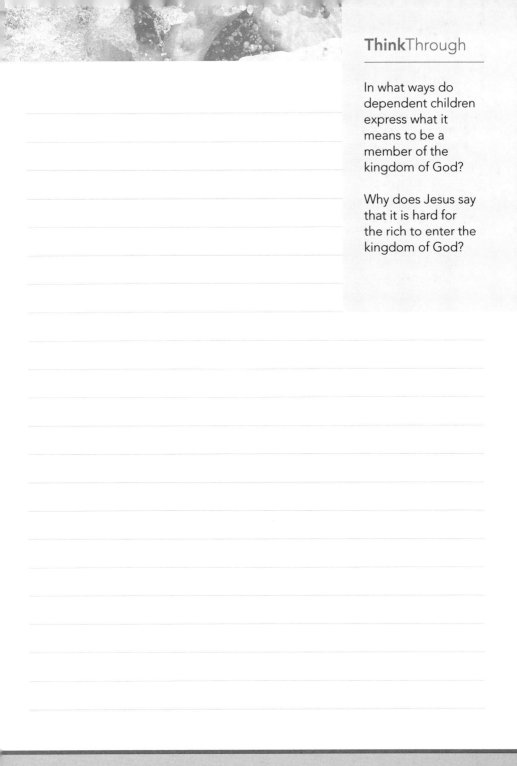

In what ways do dependent children express what it means to be a member of the kingdom of God?

Why does Jesus say that it is hard for the rich to enter the kingdom of God?

Day 48

Read Luke 19:1–10

Jesus' dramatic encounters with "little children" continue in this passage, the climactic salvation encounter in Luke's gospel.

Jesus has arrived in Jericho, just 24 kilometres from Jerusalem. There, He meets Zacchaeus. We are told two things about this man. First, he is a tax collector. Luke's gospel mentions tax collectors in association with sinners, because the two were indistinguishable in Jesus' day (Luke 5:30, 15:1). Indeed, when Zacchaeus takes Jesus home for lunch, the crowd says, "He has gone to be the guest of a sinner" (v. 7). But Zacchaeus isn't just a tax collector; he's the chief tax collector. Here in Jericho, Jesus meets the chief of sinners.

Secondly, Luke tells us that Zacchaeus is rich. He is the second rich man we have met in the space of a few verses, and Jesus has just said that it is hard for the rich to be saved. As we are about to see, though, our God is the God of the impossible (Luke 18:27).

Zacchaeus climbs a tree in an attempt to see Jesus—but, really, who is seeking whom? Jesus, without having laid eyes on this man before, knows that he is up the tree, and knows all about him. He announces to Zacchaeus that He must stay at his house (v. 5). "Must" conveys the idea that He has been sent by God to meet this chief of sinners.

Jesus and Zacchaeus have a meal together, an expression of the Lord's forgiveness and acceptance of a man whom the world despises. He announces that Zacchaeus is a true child of Abraham. Earlier, a rich ruler could not let go of his wealth (18:18–25). Now, the rich Zacchaeus demonstrates that he has found salvation by spontaneously giving away half of his money and making restitution to the people he has wronged. Zacchaeus has become completely dependent on Jesus, who can meet all his needs. He has become like a little child.

It is good to be reminded that those whom the world despises are loved by God. How encouraging: if God can save someone like Zacchaeus, then there is no one beyond His power to save. It is important to remember these truths as we pray for people.

What do we learn about true repentance from Zacchaeus' actions?

Jesus said, "The Son of Man came to seek and to save the lost" (v. 10). If this was Jesus' priority, how should that impact your life and the life of your church?

Day 49

Read Luke 19:11–27

Jesus is almost at the end of His very long journey. The next stop is Jerusalem. Before He arrives there, He tells people a story to correct any mistaken impression they might have about what is to happen.

Jews believed that when the Messiah came, He would bring salvation, which would mean both the deliverance of His people and the destruction of their enemies. This would take place at the Temple in Jerusalem, which would then become the centre of the world (e.g. Isaiah 2:1–5). Since Jesus is going to Jerusalem, the disciples could easily start thinking that the end is near. So He tells them a story to show them that what will happen in Jerusalem is not the end of God's plans for salvation, but only the beginning.

Jesus' parable is about a nobleman who goes away to receive his kingdom. He calls his slaves and gives each one a mina, which was about three to four months' wages. He tells them to "engage in business" and make a profit (v. 13).

What is this mina? It refers primarily to the money God has entrusted to us. However, Christians have seen the minas as all the gifts God gives to His people, including the greatest gift of all, which is the knowledge of the gospel. Those who are faithful in making a profit are lavishly rewarded (v. 17), while the one who is faithless is left with nothing on the day of reckoning (v. 24).

What is the profit Jesus wants from our minas? The passage begins with "While they were listening to this" (v. 11). What have the people just heard? Jesus came to seek and save the lost (v. 10). He wants us to use all He has given us to contribute to the great work of salvation in the lives of others. There will be people in the kingdom because someone shared their faith with them. There are Christians who have been blessed by our works of love (see Matthew 25:31–46).

God has given His people different minas. Whether we have received many or few, we are to use them productively. Jesus is coming back and He will want to know.

What does it mean
to "engage in
business" until Jesus
comes?

Think about the
"minas" God has
entrusted to you.
How have you been
using them for the
blessing of others?

Day 50

Read Luke 19:28–48

Finally, Jesus has arrived at His destination. He enters the last week of His life, but His exciting, triumphal march into the city gives no hint of the chaos, conflict, and suffering that are to follow.

Jesus sends two disciples ahead to collect a donkey. Showing His prophetic power, He instructs them how to reply when someone tries to stop them from taking the donkey away (vv. 30–34).

Like Solomon did almost 1,000 years before, the true King enters Jerusalem, riding on a donkey (1 Kings 1:33). Riding a donkey here isn't a symbol of Jesus' humility, as we so often think. It is an appropriate sign of His kingly power (Zechariah 9:9).

All the people lay their garments and branches on the road, praising God as they welcome their King into the city (vv. 36–38). Of course, none of them have any idea of how Jesus will come into His kingdom. It will not be by walking into the Temple carrying a sceptre, but by being nailed to a cross wearing a crown of thorns. That is why Jesus greets their praises not with laughter and smiles, but with tears and a prophecy of doom (vv. 41–44). Since they will soon kill their King who has come to save them, the days of this once-glorious city are numbered. What was their sin? They could not "recognise the time of God's coming to you" (v. 44). **Praise God, that He has opened our eyes to see Jesus, the crucified and triumphant King of Kings.**

The largest part of the Temple was the Court of the Gentiles, which covered about 26–35 acres. One section was the Temple's commercial hub. It hosted an immense volume of trade converting foreign money into shekels that were acceptable for offerings in the Temple. However, in their hunger for huge profits, the people had forgotten the Temple's true purpose: prayer and worship (v. 46).

In the book of Revelation, John sees the new Jerusalem. He writes, "I did not see a temple in the city, because the Lord God Almighty and the Lamb are its temple" (Revelation 21:22). On that day, God's true people will offer true worship to the true Temple.

Why do you think the disciples who praised Jesus as He entered Jerusalem deserted Him a few days later? Is there a lesson and warning in this for us?

How should the fact that the temple is no longer a building but "the Lord God Almighty and the Lamb", affect our understanding and practice of worship?

Day 51

Read Luke 20:1–19

Whose word can you trust? Today, many people have lost confidence in traditional authority figures like government and religion, and believe that the only person you can trust is yourself. The question of "authority" is the subject of the first verbal conflict between Jesus and the religious leaders in the Temple.

These leaders interrogate Jesus about His authority to do "these things" (v. 2). Jesus has claimed to forgive sins, to determine what happens on the Sabbath day, and to rule the Temple. Of course, only one person can declare forgiveness, determine God's law, and announce the future of the Temple, and that is God himself. Cleansing the Temple and then teaching there (Luke 19:45–47) is the latest example of Jesus exerting His divine authority.

Jesus counters their question with a question about the origin and authority of John's baptism (v. 4). The ministries of John and Jesus were intimately connected. John's first work was to prepare the way for the Lord. He announced that Jesus was the Messiah. Therefore, to acknowledge John's preaching was to submit to Jesus. This is why the leaders refuse to answer the question. They cannot deny John was sent from God, but they will not accept his testimony of Jesus.

Jesus then tells a confronting parable which summarises the historical relationship between faithless Israel and her faithful God (vv. 9–16). Isaiah 5 describes Israel as God's vineyard, and therefore all the hearers would know who Jesus is talking about. Israel persistently rejected God's prophets, and now they will kill His son.

Jesus concludes by announcing that God's vineyard will be given to others (v. 16). This introduces the idea that the new vineyard will comprise both believing Jews and Gentiles. We see here, too, the depth of the hatred of the Jewish leaders. Even after having heard Jesus announce their certain judgment, they still refuse to believe.

While this parable speaks of God's judgment on faithless Israel, it is also a story about God's amazing grace. Again and again God sent prophets to call His people to turn back to Him. Finally, He gives the greatest gift of all, His Son. **The Lord is slow to anger and abounding in love, not wanting anyone to perish** (Psalm 103:8; 2 Peter 3:9). What an encouragement to us as we pray for family and friends to turn to Jesus.

ThinkThrough

Why do you think Jesus chooses not to give the Jewish leaders a direct answer to their question, but replies with a question of His own? Are there occasions when we should follow His example?

Read Isaiah 5:1–7. What does Jesus' parable of the vineyard (vv. 9–16) tell us about God's love for His people and their response to Him? What can we learn from this parable?

Day 52

Read Luke 20:20–47

I was asked recently why I continue to follow Jesus. One of the many reasons is Jesus himself, His love, power and wisdom. In this passage, we see the wisdom of Christ as He answers more questions designed to trap Him and have Him condemn himself (v. 20).

The first question is about the Roman poll tax (vv. 21–26), which was about a day's wage. Jews hated it because it was a daily reminder that they were in captivity to a godless foreign power. If Jesus were to say, "Yes, pay it", He would turn the people against Him, but if He were to say, "Don't pay it", then He would be an enemy of Rome. Through His answer, Jesus shows us the relationship between spiritual power and secular power.

The coin bears Caesar's image, which marks it as belonging to him, just like every human being bears the image of God, and so we belong to God. Jesus demonstrates that we have obligations to the government while also affirming God's sovereignty over everything and everyone.

As Christians, we pay taxes, honour our rulers, and seek the peace and prosperity of our nation.

Yet we are also aliens and exiles, and must give our first allegiance to the King of Kings, who gives us the authority to preach the gospel and make disciples.

The Sadducees, who did not believe in the resurrection, ask a question about marriage in heaven (vv. 27–38). They make the same mistake that most people do—thinking that life in heaven will essentially be the same as life on earth, only better and longer. In effect, Jesus is saying that you can no more tell what life in heaven will be like by looking at life in this age, than you could predict what a butterfly would look like by looking at a caterpillar.

Remember that the one who has spoken to us today is much more than an earthly king. He is the eternal, glorious Son of God who sits at God's right hand and will one day make all His enemies bow before Him (vv. 41–44). These are all great reasons to keep following Jesus.

ThinkThrough

What should Christians do when our obligation to obey the government conflicts with our commitment to the Lord Jesus?

When we think about heaven, how can we make some of the mistakes we read about in this passage? What is it about heaven that should encourage and excite us as Christians?

Day 53

Read Luke 21:1–4

Jesus is still in the Temple and He has finished teaching and debating. He sits down, taking a seat opposite the treasury. There were thirteen money chests for different kinds of offerings, and Jesus is sitting and watching people. The people are throwing their money into the chests, completely unaware that the Son of God is watching everything they do.

Jesus hears the money being dropped into the chests. There is a saying that "money talks", and on that day, the money was speaking. Jesus can tell from the sound of the coins just how much people are giving. Jesus ignores the rich who are loudly giving money. Once again, a widow becomes the model of faith (see Luke 18:1–8). Jesus sees this poor, nameless woman who drops in two small copper coins that would have hardly made a sound. This coin was the least valuable of any coin in circulation.

What would that widow's coins have contributed to the upkeep of the Temple? Almost nothing—but that is not the point. God's economy is completely different from ours. This woman "put in all she had to live on" (v. 4). She is anonymous, but she has gone down in church history as one of the great examples of costly discipleship.

Perhaps it surprises us that Jesus does not go on to say, "And the woman went from there and God blessed her abundantly, and she was never in financial need again. So it will be for everyone who gives to the kingdom of God." We are not meant to think that if we give something to God, we are going to be richly repaid financially. We do not know what happened to that woman. She may have remained poor, simply trusting the Lord to provide her daily bread.

When it comes to pleasing God, no person has any advantage over another. It does not matter whether you are rich or poor. He sees the poor widow who is little in the eyes of the world but who loves the Lord so much that she gives Him everything she has. She has given us an example for us to imitate.

What does it mean that this widow "put in all she had"? What does it mean for us to put in all we have?

As we continue journeying with Jesus through Luke, we have heard Him repeatedly talk about the godly use of money and possessions. How would you summarise what Jesus has taught?

Day 54

Read Luke 21:5–38

The ancient world had seven wonders, including the Hanging Gardens of Babylon and the Colossus of Rhodes. Only one of them, the Great Pyramid of Giza, remains. Another great ancient building was the Temple of Jerusalem. It, too, has been destroyed. Nothing man-made is permanent.

In this passage, Jesus prophesies the terrible destruction of Jerusalem by the Romans in 70 AD. He teaches that the judgment that will shortly come upon Jerusalem is a mirror of the greater judgment that will come upon the whole earth at His return.

When the disciples ask Jesus when this will take place (v. 7), he first gives them the long view of human history. What Jesus says here applies to all disciples, not just those in the first century. Throughout history, many false Messiahs will come (v. 8) and there will be wars (vv. 9–10), natural disasters (v. 11), and the persecution of Christians (vv. 12–19). Both governing authorities and family members will turn against God's people, but we should not fear because while they may kill us (v. 16), Jesus assures us that "not a hair of your head will perish" (v. 18). Or, as He has already said, "do not be afraid of those who kill the body and after that can do no more . . . [for] the very hairs of your head

are all numbered" (Luke 12:4–7). God knowing the hairs of our head is a picture of our eternal security.

Then Jesus addresses the more immediate question of the fall of Jerusalem (vv. 20–24). The ancient Jewish historian, Josephus, claimed that one million died in the destruction of the city. It will be so terrible that Jesus warns people to flee. However, this destruction is a picture on a small scale of "what is coming on the world" when Jesus returns (v. 26). Just as Jesus' words were fulfilled in 70 AD, we can be sure that His prophecy for the final judgment will come to pass.

The call for Jesus' disciples in every age is not to be seduced into ungodly activities or to be so anxious about life's problems that we stop living in expectation of that day. It will come upon us suddenly and so we must remain faithful, that we "may be able to stand before the Son of Man" (v. 36).

Every day, our newspapers report wars and tragedies. Remember that these "signs", our world's death throes, are the necessary precursors for the greatest and final event in human history, the coming of the Son of Man.

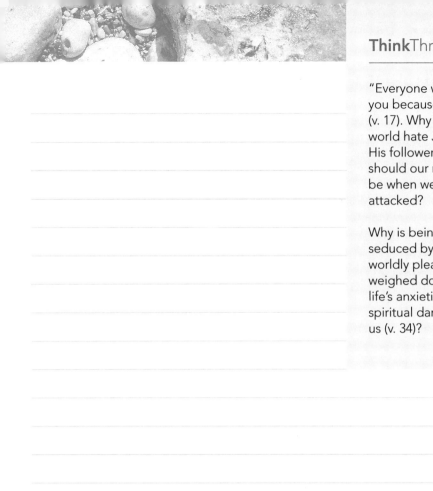

"Everyone will hate you because of me" (v. 17). Why does the world hate Jesus and His followers? What should our response be when we are attacked?

Why is being seduced by worldly pleasures or weighed down by life's anxieties such a spiritual danger for us (v. 34)?

Day 55

Read Luke 22:1–23

Almost from the very beginning of His ministry, the Jewish leaders had been plotting against Jesus (see Luke 6:11), and now they are looking for an opportunity to kill Him. His repeated humiliation of them in the Temple debates has only hardened their resolve. To arrest Him openly would incite a riot, as He is too popular. They need a time and place when Jesus can be quickly and quietly seized, and then tried and executed, but they don't know His daily timetable. They are delighted when one of His own disciples decides to betray Him (vv. 3–6).

Luke gives us two reasons for this betrayal. "Satan entered Judas" (v. 3). Satan's great work has been to destroy the mission of God's Son, and so undermine all that God is doing to bring salvation to the world. Yet that does not diminish Judas' own responsibility (v. 22). The Jews were delighted to give Judas money and, we can be sure, he was equally glad to receive it (v. 5).

There is, however, another power behind all these events. Satan's will and human will are not sovereign. Jesus says, "The Son of Man will go as it has been decreed" (v. 22). Behind these evil events of the next few days is the powerful hand of God, working through betrayal, suffering, and death to reconcile men and women to Him.

The Passover meal consisted of meat, herbs, and vegetables, but Jesus focuses on the unleavened bread and the wine, teaching the disciples their true meaning. The book of Exodus predicted that the Christ would die (Exodus 12:1–28). The broken bread looked forward to His body, and the wine symbolised His shed blood. Jesus is revealing what had always been the true meaning and intent of the Passover (see Luke 24:44–46). How appropriate that we regularly gather as His disciples and share a meal that remembers His death for us (v. 19).

We believe in an all-mighty God who wonderfully and mysteriously achieves His good purposes for our salvation by working through the deliberate, wilful choices and actions of men and women as well as the schemes of the devil. It is because we believe in the awesome sovereignty of God that we can pray with confidence and not fear the future.

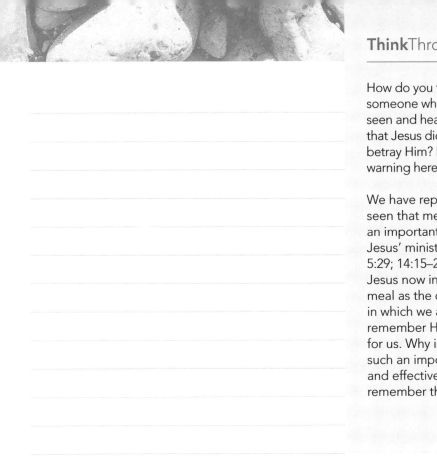

How do you think someone who had seen and heard all that Jesus did could betray Him? Is there a warning here for us?

We have repeatedly seen that meals were an important part of Jesus' ministry (Luke 5:29; 14:15–24; 15:2). Jesus now initiates a meal as the context in which we are to remember His death for us. Why is a meal such an important and effective way to remember the cross?

Day 56

Read Luke 22:24–46

Jesus taught us to pray, "Lead us not into temptation" (Luke 11:4). Now we will see how important this petition was for the disciples, Jesus himself, and us.

During the Passover meal, Jesus hears the disciples arguing about who among them was the greatest. Jesus radically redefines greatness. True greatness is marked not by displays of power but service, and Jesus himself has been the model for that.

He then warns Peter that Satan has asked for permission to test the genuineness of his faith. In the same way that God allowed Satan to test Job (Job 1), He grants the evil one permission, but Jesus assures Peter that though the disciple will briefly fail the trial (v. 34), Jesus will be upholding him throughout. Thus strengthened, Peter's ministry will be more productive as a result.

God may allow us to go through a time of sifting.

Jesus knows the plans of Satan, and so we can be encouraged that during our trials, our Lord is praying for us (see Romans 8:34). We can also be sure that the same God who restored Peter will also keep us by His mighty power (see 1 Peter 1:5).

Jesus warns the disciples that their future ministry will be a difficult one, as they will face people who will be hostile to them. Later in the Garden (vv. 49–51), they appear to take His reference to buying a sword (v. 36) literally. But Jesus will rebuke them for using one. The need for a sword is Jesus' way of warning them that the days ahead will be marked by opposition and suffering.

Jesus knows He will face the greatest trial of all. He goes to a garden called Gethsemane. It is late, and so the garden was deserted, which is why He liked it so much. He prays, asking His Father to take this cup from Him. Through Jeremiah, God said, "Take from my hand this cup filled with the wine of my wrath and make all the nations to whom I send you drink it" (Jeremiah 25:15). The cup that God has ordained for Jesus to drink is His wrath poured out on sinful people. The prospect of bearing God's anger causes Jesus terrible anguish, and so He prays for God's strength. How wonderful that Jesus drank that cup for you and me.

Can you think of times of severe testing in your life? How did the Lord sustain you through those times? How have these tough times equipped you to serve others?

What was it about His coming suffering that caused the Lord Jesus such anguish?

Day 57

Read Luke 22:47–71

The name "Judas" has become synonymous with betrayal. A kiss is an intimate and affectionate expression of love and friendship. How tragic that the only time in the Gospels when there is any record of a kiss, it is here in Judas' betrayal.

Jesus asks why He is being arrested. Do they think He is leading a rebellion (v. 52)? The great irony is that while Jesus and His followers are obedient citizens, His kingdom challenges the authority of all secular rulers. A kingdom of righteousness and renewal, whose weapons are deeds and words of love and which captures the hearts of men and women, is profoundly radical.

Luke now describes and contrasts two trials. The first is that of Peter, who follows Jesus and warms himself by the fire. In a Jewish court, a person was condemned on the evidence of three witnesses, and three witnesses testify that Peter is a disciple of Jesus (vv. 56, 58, 59). Peter loudly denies it. In that very moment, our Lord's prophetic word is fulfilled and the cock crows.

Luke then describes the mock trial of Jesus. The religious authorities have already decided that Jesus must die. They ask Him if He is the long-awaited Messiah. Jesus answers, not by denying He is the Christ, but by explaining the real character of the Christ. He is actually a divine person who will one day sit in the position of all authority (v. 69).

In contrast to Peter who denies His true identity, Jesus speaks the truth and acknowledges who He really is. Finally, the Jews have the confession they've been hoping for, and so they accuse Him of blasphemy and condemn Him (v. 71).

Can you see the irony here? The Jewish leaders will now execute Jesus, believing they have destroyed His kingdom. In fact, by His death Jesus will fulfil His prophecy about himself, as He will be exalted to His position of supreme authority at God's right hand.

Don't ever be ashamed to confess who you are. We are

followers of the Lord Jesus, who rules from heaven with all authority. Our Lord is the only true Lord, whose words are powerful and effective.

Can you think of
moments when you
might be tempted to
be silent or even deny
your relationship
with the Lord Jesus?
How can this passage
encourage you at
such moments?

Read John 21:15–19
where the resur-
rected Christ meets
Peter to restore him
to service. What does
this teach us about
sin, forgiveness, and
restoration?

Day 58

Read Luke 23:1–31

Luke now takes us on the last leg of Jesus' journey to the cross. The Roman governor Pilate interrogates Jesus, and although convinced of His innocence, will not do the just thing and acquit Him. Instead, he shifts responsibility to Herod, the tetrarch (ruler) of Galilee. Since Jesus is a Galilean, Pilate wants Herod to take control of the situation (v. 7).

Herod, who had beheaded John the Baptist, had expressed a desire to meet the miracle-working Jesus (v. 8) and be entertained. Jesus has nothing to say to someone who has no interest in spiritual matters. Yet, like Pilate, Herod finds Jesus innocent (v. 15).

Despite the fact that Jesus is innocent of any crime, the Jews are determined to see Him killed. Luke tells us that the chief priests, the rulers, and the people were there (v. 13). In other words, representatives of the entire nation are present and casting their vote against Jesus.

Three times Pilate pleads with the crowd to release this innocent man. He even offers them a cruel compromise: he will have Jesus flogged before releasing Him. Hopefully, the promise of blood will satisfy the crowd. However, they demand nothing less than the worst form of execution: crucifixion (v. 21). In the end, the loud demands of the many for execution overcome the single voice asking for justice.

The people demand the release of Barabbas in the place of Jesus (v. 18). Literally, "Barabbas" means "son of Abba"—the son of the father. Here is the people's choice: either the Father's Son who is innocent, or the father's son who is guilty. The one who gives life will die in the place of the murderer. Jesus will now take Barabbas' place on the cross, just as He took our place on the cross. **Barabbas, and we, walk free because Jesus died in our place.**

As Jesus trudges to the place of execution, along the way women weep and wail. Not everyone in Jerusalem consents to His death. Tragically, though, by committing this awful deed, the Jewish leaders have brought God's judgment upon their nation (vv. 28–31).

We have seen here today an appalling abuse of justice. Yet, at the same time, we are reminded that Jesus bore this abuse because of His incredible love for you and me.

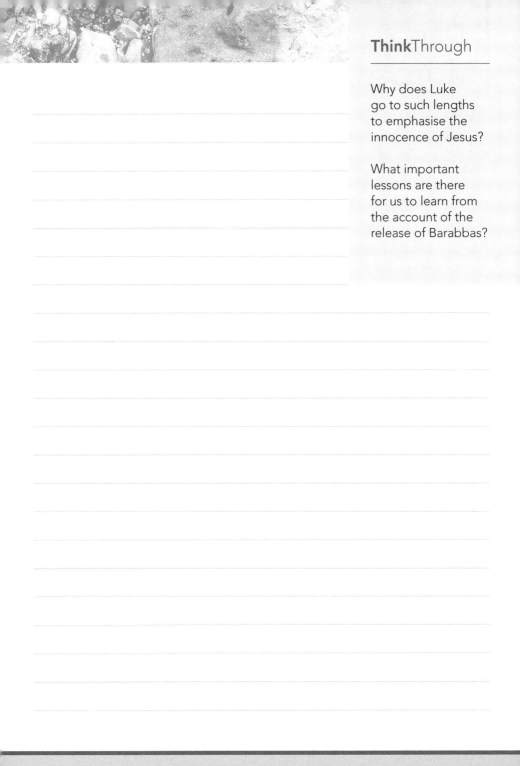

Why does Luke go to such lengths to emphasise the innocence of Jesus?

What important lessons are there for us to learn from the account of the release of Barabbas?

Day 59

Read Luke 23:32–56

Jesus now arrives at Golgotha, the place of the Skull, or, in Latin, Calvary. The people, the rulers, and the soldiers mock Him. Yet, in their mockery they proclaim the truth: "He saved others; let him save himself" (v. 35). Of course, He can only truly save others by not saving himself. The sign above the cross announces the truth: Jesus is the King of the Jews (v. 38).

Isaiah 53:12 prophesied that Jesus would be numbered with the transgressors. Luke tells us about the two criminals hanging beside Jesus. One joins the crowd in mockery, but not the other. Presumably, this man knows something about Jesus and all the good He has been doing. He has just heard Jesus ask His Father to forgive His enemies (v. 34) and understands that Jesus is innocent and is the one who can bring salvation to people. Jesus had announced, "Repent, for the kingdom of heaven has come near" (Matthew 3:2; 4:17; Mark 1:15). The thief confesses his sin (v. 41) and expresses his faith in King Jesus. As he takes his dying breath, Jesus welcomes him into His eternal kingdom. There is hope here for anyone who, even with their dying breath, sincerely turns to Christ.

As Jesus takes His final breath, there are three words of testimony. Creation speaks by bringing darkness over the land for three hours. Darkness is frequently a symbol of judgment (see Exodus 10:21; Matthew 25:30), and Jesus has borne the judgment of God that we deserved. God speaks through tearing the Temple curtain from top to bottom (v. 45). Symbolically, the Temple was the dwelling place of God, and the Almighty resided in His throne room, the Holy of Holies. Access into His presence was strictly prohibited. Once a year, the high priest could enter the Holy of Holies through the curtain (Hebrews 9:7). For anyone else, at any other time, death would be the punishment. Those days are now over! **By taking away our sin, Jesus has opened the way for all to come to God.** A Roman centurion speaks (v. 47). He has seen and heard the dying Saviour and experienced the darkness, and confesses Christ's righteous innocence.

At Jesus' birth, righteous Jews like Simeon and Anna welcomed Him. Now, at His death, a righteous Jew, Joseph, a dissenting member of the Sanhedrin, ensures Jesus is given an honourable burial (vv. 50–53).

Luke's account of Jesus' death begins with the lies and taunts of people, but ends with words of truth and faith. Whose voices will we join?

There is comfort for us in reading about the dying thief's confession of faith. However, what wrong or foolish conclusions might people draw from this story about their personal decision to turn to Christ?

What lessons about faith can we learn from the story of Joseph of Arimathea?

Day 60

Read Luke 24:1–12

For 2,000 years, Christians have woken up on Easter morning joyful, exclaiming, "Christ is risen!" Yet, on that first Easter morning, the attitude of Jesus' disciples could not have been more different. They woke up full of inconsolable sorrow (Luke 24:17; Mark 16:10).

Late on Friday, just before the Sabbath began, some of the women disciples prepare spices to anoint Jesus' body (Luke 23:55–56). With Sabbath over, they can now make the journey, at dawn's first light on Sunday morning, to pay their respects to Jesus' dead body. The last thing on their mind is that the body would not be there.

From the moment they arrive, everything is confusing. The huge stone covering the grave has been moved. The body is gone. Angels appear. None of this is making any sense to them. Then God's messengers speak: "Remember how he told you . . ." (v. 6). Seeing the empty tomb and hearing the word of God, they begin to understand.

The disciples are reluctant to believe the women's testimony. In the first-century world, a woman's testimony was given little credibility. The gospel writers would never have made up the fact that the first witnesses were women unless it was true, and they were utterly committed to faithfully recording the facts (see Luke 1:1–4).

Still, the heartbroken disciples dismiss the women's testimony that Jesus has risen as nonsense. They know that there will be a general resurrection at the end of the age, but surely no one is going to rise before then. No one has ever heard of a Messiah who would be crucified and rise from the dead. Peter, though, demonstrates the first stirrings of faith in the risen Jesus (v. 12). He has begun his road to recovery and redemption.

The cross was the world answering "no" to Jesus' claim to be the Saviour and Lord. The resurrection is God's "yes" to this claim. The resurrection of Jesus is also our guarantee that like Him, we will rise from the dead and receive our immortal, imperishable bodies, and reign with Him forever (1 Corinthians 15:20, 42–44; 2 Timothy 2:12). God will bring us, His adopted children, to resurrection life just as surely as He did His Son, Jesus.

Jesus repeatedly told the disciples that He would die and rise again. Why, then, did they fail to understand and believe when these events occurred?

If someone were to ask you how you know that Jesus really rose from the dead, what would you say?

Day 61

Read Luke 24:13–35

We now have the first of Jesus' appearances after His resurrection. Surprisingly, it is to two disciples from His wider group of disciples. These are men we have never met before and will hear nothing of again, but they are now unforgettably recorded in Biblical history.

It is still Easter Sunday and the tumultuous events of the past weekend are all that people can talk about. The disciples are both emotionally devastated that their hopes for Israel's salvation seem to have been shattered, and confused by the recent claims of the women.

These two friends are heading to Emmaus, probably their home, discussing all that has happened. To their surprise, a stranger begins to walk with them. He is Jesus although, for the moment, God keeps them from recognising Him. Their lack of physical perception matches their spiritual condition. Jesus strongly rebukes them for their failure to believe the Scriptures. They have heard the Scriptures all their lives, so how could they be so foolish as to not see that all that has happened is in fulfilment of them? He then gives them a thrilling overview of the Old Testament, showing how it all points to Him, particularly His death and resurrection.

Repeatedly, Luke has told us how important meals were in Jesus' ministry. Now, over a meal, God opens the eyes of the disciples. **The Scriptures proclaim the truth about Jesus, but it takes the enlightening of God's Spirit to bring understanding so that people can see Him and believe** (see John 16:12–15). Then Jesus disappears. Clearly, this is the same Jesus. He has walked, spoken, and eaten with them. Yet, the risen Christ is also different. This man is not under the same physical constraints that once held Him.

Immediately, the disciples run back to tell the others, only to be informed that Peter, too, has met Jesus. They then share their own testimony. This is how we meet the risen Jesus today. We read the testimonies of eyewitnesses, as recorded in the Bible; God's Spirit then takes this Word and opens the eyes of our heart to see and believe. Then we go and tell.

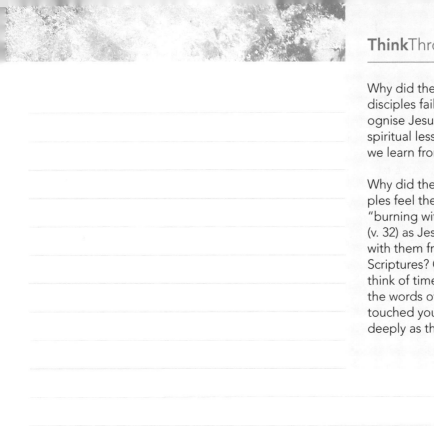

Why did these two disciples fail to recognise Jesus? What spiritual lessons can we learn from this?

Why did the disciples feel their hearts "burning within us" (v. 32) as Jesus spoke with them from the Scriptures? Can you think of times when the words of Jesus touched you as deeply as this?

Day 62

Read Luke 24:36–53

Sixty-two days ago, we began our journey through Luke. Luke began his story in the Temple in Jerusalem with a faithful priest named Zechariah (Luke 1:5). Like other Jewish saints, he was waiting for the Messiah. Appropriately, the gospel ends in the same place where it began. The faithful disciples are in the Temple praising God for sending the Messiah. However, they and all Israel have had to radically rethink their understanding of the Messiah. He is a crucified and risen Saviour.

Finally, Jesus appears to the disciples. Over the past weekend, they have betrayed Him, deserted Him, denied Him, and refused to believe eyewitnesses' testimony of His resurrection. How amazing, then, that His first words to them are a blessing, "Peace be with you" (v. 36). He can see confusion written all over their faces, and so He assures them that a ghost does not have a body and does not sit down to eat a meal with his friends. He is truly alive. His resurrection is a bodily resurrection.

To reassure them, Jesus shows them that everything that has happened was promised long ago in the Law, the Psalms, and the Prophets. He now gives them, and us, a key principle in reading and understanding the Bible. The Bible is all about Jesus.

Scripture prophesied not just that the Christ would suffer, die, and rise again for our forgiveness, but that this good news would be told to everyone (vv. 46–47). These local fishermen, tradesmen and tax collectors are sent out to the ends of the earth to proclaim this gospel. What a daunting task—but they will not be alone. Jesus will clothe them with power when He sends them His Spirit (v. 49).

We who serve Jesus in the 21st century have the same commission and the same promise: preach repentance and forgiveness of sins, and in the power of the Spirit.

Jesus' work on earth is finished. As He returns to His Father's side, His work in heaven will begin. Appropriately, the last words of Luke's gospel are, "praising God". As we conclude our amazing journey, let us pause for a moment and do just that.

Although full of joy and amazement at seeing Jesus, the disciples still have doubts and fears. Why do you think this was the case? Do we experience the same conflicting emotions today? What does Jesus do to allay their doubts (vv. 39–42)?

Having spent 62 days with Luke, write down three important things that the Lord has taught you from His Word.

Journey Through

Matthew

The first book of the New Testament makes it abundantly clear who Jesus is: the Immanuel (God with us) and Saviour of the world. It shows us how Jesus fulfills all that was predicted of the Messiah, and how His death and resurrection brings salvation and reconciles people to God. Embark on a journey of the Gospel of Matthew with Mike Raiter, and let this truth of Jesus' eternal authority change your walk with God. Be challenged as you take up Jesus' call to follow Him, and discover what it means to lead a life of total commitment to the Messiah.

Mike Raiter is a preacher, preaching trainer and former Principal of the Melbourne School of Theology in Australia. He is now Director of the Centre for Biblical Preaching and the author of a number of books, including *Stirrings of the Soul*, which won the 2004 Australian Christian Book of the Year award.

Journey Through
Mark

Take time to go through the shortest gospel in the Bible, and you'll find it packs punch. Mark's gospel presents to us the living Christ and tells us who Jesus is, what He said, and what He did. It portrays Jesus as a man of action as well as words, and reminds us how we are to love God's people in practical, compassionate ways.

Dig deeper into the book with Robert Solomon, and be amazed by what the Servant King has done for you. Follow in Jesus' footsteps, learn from His life on earth, and be led to a personal encounter with Him, so that you may become more and more like the Servant King.

Robert M. Solomon served as Bishop of The Methodist Church in Singapore from 2000–2012. He has an active itinerant preaching and teaching ministry in Singapore and abroad. He is the author of more than 30 books, including *The Race, The Conscience, The Sermon of Jesus, Faithful to the End,* and *God in Pursuit.*

ABOUT THE PUBLISHER

Since its inception in 1988, Discovery House's founding vision is to produce resources that feed the soul with the Word of God.

Since then, this publishing house has produced a wide array of quality resources that include Bible studies, video curriculum, books, music, and stationery. Each Discovery House product is designed to equip and inspire individuals in their Christian life.

Discovery House ®
from Our Daily Bread Ministries

Please direct all correspondence to the office nearest you:

Australia
Our Daily Bread Ministries
PO Box 15, Kilsyth, VIC 3137, Australia
Tel: (+61-3) 9761-7086 • Email: australia@odb.org

Hong Kong
Our Daily Bread Ministries Ltd
PO Box 74025, Kowloon Central Post Office, Kowloon, Hong Kong
Tel: (+852) 2626-1102 • Fax: (+852) 2626-0216 • Email: hongkong@odb.org

Indonesia
ODB Indonesia
PO Box 2500, Jakarta 11025, Indonesia
Tel: (+62-21) 2902-8950 • Fax: (+62-21) 5435-1975 • Email: indonesia@odb.org

Japan
Daily Bread Co Ltd
PO Box 46, Ikoma Nara 630-0291, Japan
Email: japan@odb.org

Malaysia
Our Daily Bread Berhad
PO Box 86, Taman Sri Tebrau, 80057 Johor Bahru, Malaysia
Tel: (+060-7) 353-1718 • Fax: (+060-7) 353-4439 • Email: malaysia@odb.org

New Zealand
Our Daily Bread Ministries
PO Box 303095, North Harbour, Auckland 0751, New Zealand
Tel: (+64-9) 444-4146 • Email: newzealand@odb.org

Philippines
Our Daily Bread Ministries Inc
PO Box 288, Greenhills 0410 Metro Manila
Tel: (+63-2) 705-1355 • Fax: (+63-2) 725-5058 • Email: philippines@odb.org

Taiwan
Our Daily Bread Ministries Foundation
PO Box 47-260, Taipei 10399, Taiwan ROC
Tel: (+886-2) 2585-5340 • Fax: (+886-2) 2585-5349 • Email: taiwan@odb.org

Singapore
Our Daily Bread Ministries Asia Ltd
5 Pereira Road #07-01, Asiawide Industrial Building, Singapore 368025
Tel: (+65) 6858-0900 • Fax: (+65) 6858-0400 • Email: singapore@odb.org

Sri Lanka
Our Daily Bread Ministries
PO Box 19, Dehiwala 10350, Sri Lanka
Tel: (+94-11) 272 1252 • Fax: (+94-11) 271 7626 • Email: srilanka@odb.org

NOTE TO THE READER

We invite you to share your response to the message in
this book by writing to us at
5 Pereira Road, #07-01 Asiawide Industrial Building,
Singapore 368025 or sending an email to
dhdasiapacific@dhp.org

For more information about other Discovery House
books, music, videos or DVDs, find us on the Internet at
www.dhp.org